Wheat & Gluten-Free Home Baking

Delici   Recipes for Healthy High-fibre Bread and Buns

Lola Workman

NH
NEW
HOLLAND

Published in 2012 by
New Holland Publishers
London • Sydney • Cape Town • Auckland
www.newhollandpublishers.com

Garfield House 86–88 Edgware Road London W2 2EA United Kingdom
1/66 Gibbes Street Chatswood NSW 2067 Australia
Wembley Square First Floor Solan Road Gardens Cape Town 8001 South Africa
218 Lake Road Northcote Auckland New Zealand

A catalogue record of this book is available at the British Library and the National Library of Australia.

ISBN: 9781742573656

Publisher: Fiona Schultz
Publishing director: Lliane Clarke
Designer: Stephanie Foti
Photography: R&R Publications except images listed above.
Production director: Olga Dementiev
Printer: Toppan Leefung Printing Limited

10 9 8 7 6 5 4 3 2 1

Follow New Holland Publishers on
Facebook: www.facebook.com/NewHollandPublishers

Contents

Introduction to Gluten-free Cookery

My introduction to gluten-free cookery came in 1980 when our daughter developed intolerance to wheat. Even though I was a commercially trained cook I found this type of cookery the most difficult that I had attempted, so if you are discouraged at any time take heart! Now due to 20 years of my attempts and failures there are many great recipes that you can master. I have been able to successfully make most products that can be made with wheat flour, although filo and a good puff pastry still elude me without the use of chemicals.

I avoid the use of guar and xanthan gums in my cookery as many reported cases of intolerance have come to me through the years, particularly of flatulence and irritable bowl symptoms. Soy flour is also avoided, as many allergy sufferers can't tolerate soy products. My superfine flour blend used in this book is also free of corn.

One of my methods is to blend your own gluten-free flour before commencing to cook. It is much less wearying if this is done on a day when you are not intending to bake. Make at least three kilos at a time, store it in a calico bag and it will keep for months; on page 7. This flour can be used for all purposes that you would normally use plain flour for. Your own flour mix will cost less than half the price of commercially packed products that can contain soy flour and unspecified ingredients such as wheat starch.

Successful gluten-free cookery is dependant on following a few important rules. Please follow the directions as each recipe has been made at least three times, sometimes six or seven times to achieve a good result. Weigh all dry ingredients using a small accurate set of scales or a digital set. Cup measurements are not good enough for this type of cookery due to the differing amounts of moisture contained in the flours and the size of the grind of the flour. If you are using rice flour, it is manufactured in many different grinds from a course ground rice to the finest powdered rice flour. Of course, 1 cup of a heavy grind weighs twice as much as a fine powdered product, hence needing more liquid and more oil or butter to prevent a crumbly product.

Carefully read the page on bread tins (page 8), this is an important part of all good cookery. Expensive utensils are not required for good results apart from an electric mixer and a good reliable oven. With a little confidence you can become a superb gluten-free cook.

Working With Your Intolerance

Be positive and work with the foods you can tolerate.

It is important to recognise and memorise the list of foods that can be included in your diet. Your dietician or doctor will provide this. Once you have this information you will soon become accustomed to reading the labels of every product that you buy. Never buy a mixed product, such as gluten-free flour, that does not specify the ingredients. In some countries, it is law that such products must contain this information. A product may be gluten-free, but can still include milk products or chemicals that you cannot tolerate.

Using my recipes in conjunction with the list of substitutes on page 9 you will be able to make almost every product gluten-free, that you could previously cook with wheat flour. If you have not tried to make such things as breads abd buns previously don't let this worry you, just follow the instructions step by step for success.

Do remember when you are making bread that homemade bread is not meant to keep fresh more than one day; if you remember, in years gone by bread was cooked every day and in country areas it still is.

The ingredients that are added to commercial breads to extend the shelf life are chemicals and additional gluten. If you are gluten intolerant these ingredients are a problem for you.

You will find that once you organise yourself to bake gluten-free foods, you will enjoy the challenge of producing fresh chemical-free foods. Bread mixes can be weighed in loaf quantities, bagged and kept in your cupboard until you are ready to bake. You can do the same thing with cookie or pastry mixes. When you are blending your own flour, always mix at least three kilos at a time and store it in a large calico bag then it will keep indefinitely for you. It has been tested here for four years without signs of rancidity.

Psyllium is used in my recipes to add elasticity and fibre that is so important in a gluten-free diet particularly where gums are regularly used. Fibre is not a laxative, as a jelly-like substance it collects seeds and hard pieces of food from the intestine that can cause inflammation easily removing them without the scouring of laxatives.

Essential Utensils

There are a few utensils I consider essential for successfully baking gluten-free, wheat-free, breads. These can be found in kitchenware shops and department stores throughout the world. I am not listing such obvious utensils as bowls, spoons and tea towels.

SCALES

A good set of scales is an essential tool; in class we use small sets of diet scales, capable of accurately weighing small quantities. Gluten-free flours vary in their moisture content depending on the area the grain is grown in and the size of the grind, consequently varying in their weight. This means that a cup of the same flour such as rice flour may weigh up to a third more depending on how finely it is ground, hence absorbing more or less liquid and giving an inconsistent result. Measuring by cup is a sure way to obtain an inconsistent result. Commercial cooks weigh every ingredient including egg pulp.

ELECTRIC MIXER

They vary depending on the size of the loaf and the regularity of your baking needs. For example, if you are cooking bread for one person, a small electric hand mixer is adequate. If you are cooking a large family-sized loaf three times a week then a large electric mixer would be necessary to avoid this becoming a tedious chore.

METRIC MEASURING CUPS

My recipes use a 250mL (9fl oz) metric measuring cup. These sets are cheap to buy and available in most countries—they should only be used for liquids.

METRIC MEASURING SPOONS

Metric measuring spoons are available in sets. My recipes use the 20mL ($^2/_3$fl oz) tablespoon. Check your tablespoon weight as many (American, British and sometimes Asian) are 15mL (½fl oz). This does not matter if you are aware of it and use a little extra to add the extra teaspoon needed. All spoon measurements are level in my recipes.

LARGE PASTA STRAINER

I use this large strainer as a sieve to easily sift ingredients and avoid contamination by the use of rotary sieves that are difficult to clean.

OVEN THERMOMETER

To establish that your oven is baking at the correct temperature.

WIRE WHISK

It is helpful to have a wire balloon whisk in your kitchen for hand blending of coarse grains that are difficult to sift.

SERRATED KNIFE

Used for slicing your bread before freezing. An electric knife is helpful.

PASTRY BRUSH, SILICONE BAKING PAPER

These are usually found in every kitchen. Silicone baking paper can be used more than once. Rinse under a cold tap and dry with a cloth.

Blending Your Own Flour

This flour was especially formulated to simplify bread-making for allergy sufferers. It has been used regularly in my gluten-free cookery classes. The blend is free of wheat, gluten, soy and corn and is suitable for all the recipes in this book. It can be used instead of my bread and pastry flour in recipes although it is lighter flour.

Lola's Superfine Flour

400g (14oz) BESAN FLOUR (Known also as chickpea/gram/channa/dhal flour)
400g (14oz) POTATO FLOUR (Sometimes called potato starch)
200g (7oz) FINE RICE FLOUR (Use the finest grind you can find)
300g (10½oz) ARROWROOT (Tapioca starch can be used instead of arrowroot)

Method: Easy Blending

You need two large plastic bags and a pasta or sauce strainer about 20cm (7¾in) in diameter.
1. Weigh the ingredients and toss them into a large plastic bag.
2. Give the bag a good shake.
3. Place the strainer in the second bag.
4. Tip the flour into the strainer in the bag and shake the strainer to sift it.

The flour is now ready for use.
Store it in a paper or calico bag so that the flour can breathe.
Stored this way the flour will keep in good condition for several years.
Do not keep this flour airtight or it will quickly become rancid.
A loose-lidded container is suitable as long as the flour can obtain some air.

Collecting Bread Tins

BREAD TINS
Should be the heaviest quality that you can find. Do not wash your bread tins more than necessary; wipe out with oiled cloth or paper. Bakers will never let their favourite tins be washed. Never put your tins in the washing machine, as strong dishwasher detergents will soon ruin good surfaces.

AVOID ALUMINIUM
It is extremely important to use good quality tins to bake gluten-free products. Aluminium baking trays will not cook these goods well as the heat is deflected instead of penetrating the tin. This action causes a thick crust on bread with a soggy uncooked centre. Cakes need a longer cooking time in aluminium that results in a dry crumbly cake as the outside of the cake cooks before the centre.

NON-STICK SURFACES
Baking trays and tins need not be expensive; non-stick surfaced pans, as long as they are not aluminium, cook cakes and muffins well. However, remember that a more expensive pan usually means the pan has a longer-lasting finish. I am still using my grandfather's bread tins, so good tins will last you a long time. Wash and dry your tins and then return them to the warm oven to dry completely.

SHAPES TO LOOK FOR
As gluten-free bread mixture is usually a batter it is necessary to have tins that will give the bread some shape. Look for ring tins with a patterned bottom or fancy shaped tin moulds such as pâté moulds. Saddle log tins used for German Christmas logs have a ribbed bottom that I grease and liberally coat with seeds to provide an interesting shape when turned out. I use these tins for my potato bread as well as bun recipes. Easter buns can be cooked in giant muffin tins and Yorkshire pudding pans make good tins for hamburger buns. Individual pie pans can be used for filled buns.

TINS FOR FLATBREADS
You can achieve a good result using a rectangular slice tin for focaccia and yeasted filled flatbreads; again make sure that it is tin.

CERAMIC TILES
I have had great success using ceramic tiles in my oven to cook flatbread. Place the tile on an oven rack and preheat it along with the oven to the required temperature. I use baking paper cut to a round or oblong shape on the tile to guide the flatbread shape as we are working with a batter mix for our gluten-free bread.

BABY RUSKS AND SAVOURY STICKS
These need tins such as sponge finger or éclair trays to give a good result.

CHILDREN'S CAKE TINS
These can be great for making school sandwiches; tins such as teddy bear or duck shaped tins give a child something different to take to school.

MINIATURE LOAF TINS
Are widely available and again good for lunches.

Substitutes

If you are missing an ingredient from a recipe, or have found that a product is troublesome to you, try a substitute.

DAIRY INTOLERANCE	Milk powder in my recipes can be replaced by extra gluten-free flour. Milk-free margarines are widely available and may be used.
CHICKPEA FLOUR	Often called besan, gram or channa dhal flour, chickpea flour can be exchanged for lupin flour or other legume flours. Beware of soya bean flour, as many people are intolerant to soy products. Yellow pea flour is sometimes bitter.
COCOA	Carob can be used instead of cocoa.
COCONUT	May be replaced with baby rice cereal and coconut essence.
CORN PRODUCTS	Corn is avoided if my flour blend (page 7) is used throughout the book and the few recipes such as cornbreads are avoided.
DRIED FRUITS	Natural dried fruits that are unsulphured are available from health food shops. A dehydrator is a valuable appliance if you can't find unsulphured dried fruit.
EGGS	There are many egg replacements on the market worldwide. I have used several of them quite successfully but find that about double the recommended amount is required for a good result; also warm water is better than cold for mixing.
GELATINE	May be replaced by agar-agar if desired. As a powder or granules agar-agar should be used at the same rate as gelatine. Leaf agar should be soaked and made a jelly by heating the soaked plant. Cool and refrigerate the jelly and use at double the gelatine rate.
SUGAR	Sugar when used to 'feed' yeast in this book should not be substituted by artificial sweeteners. If the sugar is used as a sweetening agent (ie over apples in a bun recipe) then cooking sweeteners may be used as a replacement.
SEEDS	May be replaced by other garnishes such as coarse salt, bacon or pepper.
VINEGAR	Malt vinegar is not gluten-free. Use wine, cider, rice or balsamic vinegar.
PARISIAN ESSENCE	Colouring that can be replaced with carob or white sugar heated to caramel.
PSYLLIUM	May be replaced with baby rice cereal but this will not provide the fibre and elasticity of psyllium.

Beautiful Buns

Basic Bun Dough

This easy bun mixture is used to make many different buns. If you find it a little sticky when kneading use a sprinkle of fine rice flour. The dough should be as soft as possible to make a light bun.

Ingredients

200ml (7fl oz) cold water
1 tbsp gelatine
1 tbsp psyllium
2 tbsp sugar
1 tsp salt
2 tbsp glycerine
1 tbsp dried yeast
450g (16oz) Lola's superfine flour
   (page 7)
1 egg
1 tbsp mixed spice (optional)
2 tbsp soft margarine

Preparation

- Place water in a microwave bowl and sprinkle the gelatine and psyllium on top.
- Leave to stand for a few minutes to soften.
- Heat for 40 seconds in microwave on high heat.
- Remove from heat. Add sugar, salt, glycerine and yeast, and stir to mix.
- Cover and stand for 20 minutes until mixture is doubled.
- Oil a sheet of plastic about 300 x 220mm (11¾ x 8½in).

Mixing

- Using an electric mixer whisk about three-quarters of the flour into the yeast mixture.
- Add the egg, spice and margarine and beat until a smooth batter.
- Cover and stand again for 20 minutes, then beat again for 1 minute.
- Using a spatula fold in the remaining flour and tip onto the plastic sheet.
- Lightly knead using a little fine rice flour if required.
- Use as directed.

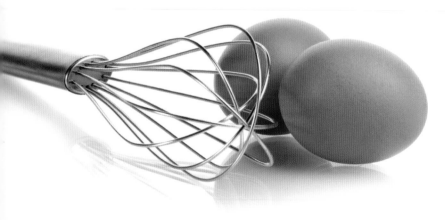

Almond and Apricot Flats

Free of wheat, gluten, dairy and oil. One medium-sized potato produces approximately 60g (2oz) mashed potato. I use large muffin tins.

Ingredients

200mL (7fl oz) cold water
1 tsp salt
2 tbsp caster (superfine) sugar
1 tbsp gelatine
60g (2oz) mashed potato
1 tbsp dried yeast
250g (8½oz) Lola's superfine flour (page 7)
20g (²/₃oz) almond meal (flour)
2 eggs
50g (2oz) chopped dried apricots
50g (2oz) flaked almonds

Preparation

- Place the cold water in a large glass bowl or microwave dish.
- Add the salt, caster sugar and gelatine.
- Let stand for 1 minute to soften gelatine.
- Heat the gelatine mixture in the microwave on high for 50 seconds.
- Grease large muffin tins with some dairy-free margarine.

Mixing

- Whisk the mashed potato into the warm gelatine mixture. Stir in the yeast and whisk slightly.
- Let stand for 3 minutes.
- Combine flour and almond meal.
- Lightly whisk the eggs with an electric mixer.
- Tip the dry ingredients into the yeast mixture and beat in the whisked eggs.
- Beat the mixture for 1 minute with the electric mixer.

Baking

- Preheat oven to 180°C (350°F).
- Pour ¼ cup of the mixture into each muffin pan and spread over the base.
- Sprinkle some of the apricot and almonds over the mixture and top with more mixture.
- Leaving aside some almonds to sprinkle over the top of each muffin, sprinkle the remaining fruit over the mixture.
- Cover with the remaining mixture and top with almonds.
- Leave to stand 15 minutes until a few bubbles appear.
- Place in the centre of the oven and bake for 15 minutes.
- Remove from the oven and wrap in a clean tea towel to cool.

Apple and Sultana Spice Ring

Ingredients

200mL (7fl oz) cold water
1 tsp salt
2 tbsp caster (superfine) sugar
1 tbsp gelatine
60g (2oz) mashed potato
1 tbsp dried yeast
250g (8½oz) Lola's superfine flour
  (page 7)
1 tsp ground ginger
1 tsp mixed spice
1 tsp ground cinnamon
2 eggs
1 cup sultanas
1 medium apple, peeled and chopped

Topping

2 cups pure icing (confectioners')
  sugar
3 tbsp margarine
Walnuts, to decorate

Preparation

- Place the cold water in a large glass bowl or microwave dish.
- Add the salt, caster sugar and gelatine. Let stand for 1 minute to soften gelatine.
- Heat the gelatine mixture in the microwave on high for 50 seconds.
- Grease a long saddle or ring pan with some dairy-free margarine.

Mixing

- Whisk the mashed potato into the warm gelatine mixture.
- Stir in the yeast and whisk slightly. Let stand for 3 minutes.
- Combine flour and spices.
- Lightly whisk the eggs with an electric mixer.
- Tip the dry ingredients into the yeast mixture and beat in the eggs.
- Beat the mixture for 1 minute with the electric mixer.

Baking

- Preheat the oven to 180°C (350°F).
- Pour a quarter of the mixture into the pan and spread over the base.
- Sprinkle a quarter of the sultanas and apple over the mixture and top with more batter.
- Sprinkle over the remaining fruit and cover with more mixture.
- Leave to stand for 15 minutes until a few bubbles appear.
- Place in the centre of the oven and bake for 35 minutes.
- Remove from the oven and wrap in a clean tea towel to cool.

Finishing

- Cream together icing sugar and margarine, adding a little hot water if necessary. Ice the cake when cool, and decorate with walnuts.

Banana and Blueberry Muffins

These yeasted muffins are well worth the extra standing time needed to raise the yeast. Yeast cookery takes a little longer so it is a good idea to make use of the time in the kitchen by making cookies or a pie while the yeast is rising.

Ingredients

200mL (7fl oz) milk
1 tsp salt
1 tbsp gelatine
100g (4oz) caster (superfine) sugar
1 tbsp dried yeast
2 eggs
1 ripe banana
2 tbsp rice syrup or honey
2 tbsp olive oil
160g (5½oz) Lola's superfine flour (page 7)
1 tbsp psyllium
150g (1 cup) fresh blueberries

Preparation

- Place milk in a large microwave-proof mixing bowl.
- Add salt, gelatine and 1 tablespoon of the caster sugar.
- Let stand for a few minutes, and then heat in microwave for 1 minute on high.
- Grease a 12-cup muffin tin or line with paper cases.

Mixing

- Stir the yeast into the warm milk mixture and leave to stand for 20 minutes.
- Lightly beat the eggs. In a small bowl, mash the banana and add the rice syrup, olive oil and eggs. Blend this mixture until smooth.
- Combine the two wet mixes in the large bowl and add the flour, psyllium, and remaining caster sugar.
- Mix well, cover the bowl and leave to rise for 20 minutes.
- Fold in the blueberries and spoon the mixture into the muffin tins.
- Leave to rise for another 20 minutes before baking.

Baking

- Preheat the oven to 180°C (350°F).
- Bake muffins for 30 minutes.

Chocolate Chip Buns

Ingredients

200mL (7fl oz) cold water
1 tbsp gelatine
1 tbsp psyllium
2 tbsp glycerine
4 tbsp sugar
½ tsp salt
1 tbsp dried yeast
350g (12oz) Lola's superfine flour
  (page 7)
2 tbsp sifted cocoa
1 egg
2 tbsp soft margarine
100g (4oz) dark chocolate chips

Bun Glaze

1 tsp gelatine
2 tbsp sugar
2 tbsp water

Preparation

- Place water in a microwave bowl and sprinkle the gelatine and psyllium on top.
- Leave to stand for a few minutes to soften, and then heat for 1 minute in microwave on high heat
- Remove from heat and add the glycerine, sugar, salt and yeast. Stir to mix.
- Cover and stand for 20 minutes.
- Grease a 12-cup muffin tin with the extra margarine.

Mixing

- Add the flour, cocoa, egg and margarine to the yeast mixture.
- Using an electric mixer beat for 3 minutes.
- Cover and stand again for 20 minutes.
- Beat again for 1 minute and spoon 1 tablespoon of mixture into each muffin cup.
- Top the mixture with some chocolate chips.
- Add more mixture to cover the chocolate.
- Leave to rise for 20 minutes.

Baking

- Preheat the oven to 200°C (400°F).
- When the buns have risen, reduce the oven temperature to 180°c.
- Bake for 15 minutes, remove from oven and glaze while hot.
- Bun glaze
- Boil ingredients together and brush on to hot buns.

Cinnamon Cross Buns

Makes six large buns (without fruit) baked in large muffin tins.

Ingredients

1 cup cold water
2 tsp salt
150g (5oz) caster (superfine) sugar
1 tsp psyllium
1 tbsp gelatine
1 tbsp glycerine
2 tbsp margarine
2 tbsp dried yeast
400g (14oz) Lola's superfine flour
  (page 7)
60g (2oz) baby rice cereal
60g (2oz) almond meal
2 tsp mixed spice
1 tsp ground cinnamon
1 tsp ground ginger
2 egg whites

Bun Glaze

1 tsp gelatine
2 tbsp sugar
2 tbsp water

Preparation

- Place the cold water, salt,
  1 teaspoon of the sugar, psyllium
  and gelatine in a large glass
  bowl or microwave dish. Let
  stand for 1 minute to soften.
- Heat in the microwave for 40
  seconds. Grease muffin tins with
  some margarine.

Mixing

- Add the glycerine and margarine to the warm gelatine mixture.
- Stir in the yeast and whisk slightly. Let stand for 3 minutes.
- Place flour, baby rice cereal, almond meal and spices in a
  plastic bag and give a good shake to mix well.
- Whisk the egg whites and remaining sugar until stiff.
- Add the yeast mixture to the meringue and tip in the dry
  ingredients.
- Beat the mixture for 2 minutes with the electric mixer.
- Let stand for 10 minutes. Whisk for 30 seconds.
- For easier filling of muffin tins, pour the mixture into a jug to fill
  the tins.

Baking

- Preheat oven to 180°C (350°F). Leave the mixture to stand for
  15 minutes until a few bubbles appear.
- Pipe crosses on top of each bun.
- Place in the centre of the oven and bake for 30 minutes.
- Glaze while they are still hot.

Cross mix

- Sprinkle 2 teaspoon of psyllium on ¼ cup cold water and let
  stand to thicken. Add 1 tablespoon sugar and 1 tablespoon
  fine rice flour. Pipe on the uncooked buns.

Bun glaze
- Boil ingredients together and brush on to hot buns.

Crown of Thorns

Laden with fruit and nuts, this is perfect for Easter.

Ingredients

1 batch of basic bun dough (page 12)

Filling

30g (1oz) margarine
100g (4oz) raisins
100g (4oz) sultanas
30g (1oz) mixed peel

Topping

½ cup slivered almonds
1 tbsp ground cinnamon
1 tbsp ground ginger
1 tbsp caster (superfine) sugar
2 tbsp ground almonds
2 tbsp brown sugar
1 egg yolk

Glaze

1 egg white
1 tbsp caster (superfine) sugar

To Assemble

- Press the dough out to the size of a plastic sheet 300 x 220mm (11¾ x 8½in).
- Spread with the margarine and sprinkle evenly with fruit.
- Roll the dough up lengthwise using the plastic sheet to help.
- Form a circle on a greased tray or in a shallow ring tin.
- Snip at intervals with sharp scissors.
- Leave to rise for 30 minutes.

Baking

- Preheat the oven to 180°C (350°F).
- Setting aside the silvered almonds, mix the topping ingredients together; if too stiff add a little of the egg white.
- Spread evenly on top of the risen dough.
- Arrange the almonds to form thorns around the crown. Bake for 30 minutes
- Remove from oven and glaze with the egg white and sugar mixture.
- Return to the oven for 5 minutes.
- Serve warm.

Currant and Custard Scrolls

Ingredients

1 batch of basic bun dough (page 12)
½ cup currants

Custard

2 tbsp margarine
2 tbsp Lola's superfine flour (page 7)
½ cup boiling water
1 egg yolk
½ cup sugar
Vanilla essence to taste
3 tbsp almond meal

Preparation

- Make the custard and set aside to cool.
- Oil a sheet of plastic about 300 x 220mm (11¾ x 8½in).
- Cover a baking tray with silicone baking paper.
- Press the dough out to the size of the plastic sheet.
- Spread with the custard filling, and sprinkle with currants.
- Roll the dough up lengthwise using the plastic sheet to help.
- Using an oiled knife, cut the scrolls in thick slices and place on the prepared tray.

Baking

- Preheat the oven to 180°C (350°F).
- Leave the scrolls to rise for 20 minutes.
- Bake for 15 minutes.
- Remove from oven and glaze while hot.

To make the custard

- Melt the margarine in a small saucepan and add the flour. Cook for 1 minute stirring with a wooden spoon.
- Add the boiling water and cook until the custard is thick.
- Add the egg yolk, sugar, vanilla and almond meal, and stir well.
- It should be thick enough to hold its shape, if not add a little more almond meal.

Bun glaze

- Boil ingredients together and brush on to hot buns.

Easy Cinnamon Teacake

I cook this cake in a 20cm (7¾in) sponge tin. It can be precooked, wrapped in foil, and just warmed in microwave to serve.

Ingredients

1 egg
100g (4oz) sugar
1 tbsp boiling water
1 tbsp margarine
1 tsp vanilla essence
125mL (4fl oz) milk
140g (5oz) Lola's superfine flour
   (page 7)
2 tsp ground cinnamon
1 tbsp almond meal
1 tsp gelatine
2 tsp gluten-free baking powder

Preparation

- Grease a 20cm sponge tin with margarine and line the bottom with a circle of greaseproof or baking paper.
- Place the egg and sugar in a medium bowl and hand whisk over hot water for about 1 minute until just warm. (this hastens the beating of the egg and sugar.)
- Take a tablespoon of boiling water from the saucepan and place in a cup with the margarine.
- Add the vanilla essence.
- Preheat the oven to 180°C (350°F).

Mixing

- Using an electric mixer beat the warm egg and sugar mixture until thick.
- Add the milk and margarine water mixture to the egg mixture by pouring it down the side of the bowl (so not to flatten the egg mixture).
- Using a wire whisk lightly fold in the flour, cinnamon, almond meal, gelatine and baking powder.

Baking

- Pour the mixture into the prepared pan.
- Bake for 25 minutes until firm and springy.
- Serve warm with butter.

Date and Walnut Roll

Use a roll tin approximately 8cm (3in) in diameter and 16cm (6in) high.

Ingredients

125mL (4fl oz) milk
1 cup chopped dates
½ cup chopped walnuts
3 tbsp margarine
200g (7oz) Lola's superfine flour
   (page 7)
2 tbsp caster (superfine) sugar
2 tsp gluten-free baking powder
1 tsp mixed spice
1 tbsp ground cinnamon
1 egg

Preparation

- Grease a long roll tin with margarine and sprinkle with a little flour.
- Preheat the oven to 180°C (350°F).

Mixing

- Place the milk in a large mixing bowl; add the dates, walnuts and margarine.
- Combine flour, sugar, baking powder and spices.
- Tip the dry ingredients into the milk mixture.
- Add the egg and beat with a wooden spoon for about 1 minute.
- Spoon into the prepared roll tin.

Baking

- Place in the centre of the oven and bake for 25 minutes.
- Remove from the oven and wrap in a clean tea towel to cool.
- Serve warm.

Date and Linseed Loaf

Use a 20cm (7¾in) ring or 30cm (11¾in) saddle or log tin.

Ingredients

125mL (4fl oz) cold water
1 tsp salt
2 tbsp caster (superfine) sugar
2 tsp psyllium
2 tsp parisian essence
1 tbsp liquid glucose
2 tsp gelatine
2 tbsp linseeds
1 tbsp dried yeast
200g (7oz) Lola's superfine flour
   (page 7)
1 tbsp mixed spice
1 tbsp ground cinnamon
1 tbsp carob
1 egg
2 tbsp olive oil
100g (4oz) chopped dates

Preparation

- Place the cold water in a large glass bowl or microwave dish.
- Add the salt, caster sugar, psyllium, parisian essence, liquid glucose and gelatine.
- Let stand for 1 minute to soften gelatine.
- Heat the mixture in the microwave on high for 50 seconds.
- Grease a long saddle or ring pan with dairy-free margarine and sprinkle with 1 tablespoon of the linseeds.

Mixing

- Remove the mixture from microwave.
- Stir in the yeast and whisk slightly. Let stand for 10 minutes.
- Combine flour, spices, carob and remaining linseeds; dry whisk to blend.
- Tip the dry ingredients into the yeast mixture.
- Add the egg and oil and beat with an electric mixer for about 1 minute.
- Cover and let rise for 20 minutes.
- Beat again and fold in the chopped dates .
- Spoon into the prepared baking pan, cover and leave again for 20 minutes.

Baking

- While the loaf is standing, preheat the oven to 180°C (350°F).
- Place in the centre of the oven and bake for 30 minutes.
- Remove from the oven and wrap in a clean tea towel to cool.
- Serve warm spread with butter.

Iced Finger Buns

Éclair trays are used to cook these buns.

Ingrendients

1 batch of basic bun Dough (page 12)

Pink Icing

1 cup pure icing (confectioners') sugar
2 tsp margarine
little warm water
pink food colour

Preparation

- Oil a sheet of plastic about 300 x 220mm (11¾ x 8½in).
- Grease the éclair trays with margarine.

Assembly

- Press the dough out to the size of the plastic sheet.
- Fold the dough in three lengthwise using the plastic sheet to help.
- Using an oiled knife, cut the bun dough in thick slices.
- Place in greased éclair tray and leave to rise for 20 minutes.

Baking

- Preheat the oven to 180°C (350°F).
- Bake for 15 minutes.

Pink Icing

- Blend together and spread over the bun tops.

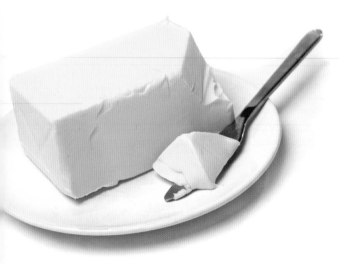

My German Teacake

I cook this cake in a 20cm (7¾in) sponge tin. It can be precooked, wrapped in foil, and just warmed in the microwave to serve.It's great for suppers when you have to take a plate.

Ingrendients

2 eggs
250g (8½oz) Lola's superfine flour
   (page 7)
2 tsp gluten-free baking powder
1 tsp gelatine
30g (1oz) margarine
½ tsp salt
100g (4oz) sugar
½ cup milk

Topping

egg yolk
1 tbsp brown sugar
1 tbsp almond meal
2 tsp ground cinnamon

Preparation

- Grease a 20cm sponge pan with margarine, and line the bottom with a circle of greaseproof or baking paper.
- Separate the eggs, placing the whites in a large mixing bowl and the yolks in separate small dishes.
- Weigh the flour and add the baking powder and gelatine to it.
- Melt the margarine in a cup in the microwave for 20 seconds.
- Prepare the topping by combining all the topping ingredients in a small bowl.
- Preheat oven to 180°C (350°F).

Mixing

- Whisk the egg whites, salt and sugar until stiff.
- Stir in one egg yolk, and the milk.
- Add the dry ingredients and the melted butter.
- Whisk well to mix.

Baking

- Pour the mixture into the prepared pan and drop the topping on top in small nut-sized pieces.
- Bake for 25 minutes until firm and springy.
- Serve warm with butter.

Pixie Custard Buns

Ingredients

1 batch of basic bun Dough (page 12)
½ cup sultanas
1 red apple, sliced

Custard filling

1 tbsp margarine
1 tbsp Lola's Superfine Flour (page 7)
½ cup boiling water
2 tbsp sugar
2 tbsp vanilla essence
4 tbsp cream cheese
2 tbsp ground almonds

Preparation

You will need two sheets of plastic about 300 x 220mm (11¾ x 8½in).

- Grease the pixie bun trays and make the custard filling.

Assembly

- Press the dough out between the plastic sheets.
- Cut out circles with a large serrated cutter and press lightly into the pans, making sure that the dough comes up to the top of the pan.
- Place a few sultanas in the bun and spoon on a tablespoon of custard.
- Top with a few slices of red apple before sealing with a lid of bun dough. Use a smaller cutter for the lids and drop the lids into a saucer of cold water before placing on top of the filled bun. (This will seal in the custard.)

Baking

- Leave to rise for 30 minutes before baking for 15 minutes.
- Preheat oven to 180°C (350°F).

To make the custard

- Melt the margarine in a saucepan, add the flour and cook for 1 minute.
- Add the water and whisk over heat until thick.
- Whisk in the sugar, vanilla essence, cream cheese and ground almonds.
- Place in the refrigerator to cool.
Note: Custard can be made the previous day.

Seeded Honey Loaf

Use a 16cm-round high tin for this loaf.

Ingredients

125mL (4fl oz) water
1 tsp salt
2 tbsp caster (superfine) sugar
2 tsp psyllium
¼ cup honey
1 tbsp treacle
2 tsp gelatine
2 tbsp poppy seeds
1 tbsp dried yeast
250g (8½oz) Lola's superfine flour
  (page 7)
1 tsp ground cinnamon
1 eggs
2 tbsp olive oil

Preparation

- Place the cold water in a large glass bowl or microwave dish.
- Add the salt, caster sugar, psyllium, honey, treacle and gelatine.
- Let stand for 1 minute to soften gelatine.
- Heat the mixture in the microwave on high for 1 minute.
- Grease a high bun tin with margarine and sprinkle with 1tablespoon of the poppy seeds.

Mixing

- Remove the mixture from microwave.
- Stir in the yeast and whisk slightly. Let stand for 20 minutes.
- Combine flour, cinnamon, and remaining poppy seeds.
- Tip the dry ingredients into the yeast mixture.
- Add the egg and oil and beat with an electric mixer for about 1 minute.
- Cover and let rise for 20 minutes. Whisk for another minute.
- Spoon into the prepared baking pan, cover and leave again for 30 minutes.

Baking

- Preheat oven to 150°C (300°F).
- Place the tin in the centre of the oven and bake for 1 hour.
- Remove from the oven and wrap in a clean tea towel to cool.
- Serve warm spread with butter.

Spicy Pull-aparts

I cook these easy buns on a scone tray or in a slice tin. Some fine rice flour in a shaker may be needed for rolling but don't add too much as this will dry the pull-aparts.

Ingredients

1 batch of basic bun dough (page 12)
1 cup sultanas
1 tbsp brown sugar
2 tsp mixed spice

Bun Glaze

1 tsp gelatine
2 tbsp sugar
2 tbsp water

Preparation

- Oil a sheet of plastic about 300 x 220mm (11¾ x 8½in).
- Line a scone tray with baking paper.

Assembly

- Using the plastic sheet as a guide, press out the dough in an oblong shape to cover the sheet. Sprinkle the dough with brown sugar, spice and fruit.
- Roll up lengthwise using the oiled plastic to help.
- Using an oiled knife, slice the roll into bun-sized pieces.
- Place the pieces on the scone tray.

Baking

- Preheat the oven to 180°C (350°F).
- Set the pull-aparts aside for 20 minutes to rise.
- Bake for 15 minutes.
- Glaze with bun glaze while hot.

Bun Glaze

- Boil ingredients together and brush on to hot buns.

Walnut and Raspberry Jam Scrolls

Ingredients

1 batch of Basic Bun Dough (page 12)
¼ cup raspberry jam
100g (4oz) walnut halves

Bun Glaze

1 tsp raspberry jam
1 tsp gelatine
2 tbsp sugar
2 tbsp water

Preparation

- Oil a sheet of plastic about 300 x 220mm (11¾ x 8½in).
- Cover a baking tray with silicone baking paper.

Assembly

- Press the dough out to the size of the plastic sheet.
- Spread the raspberry jam on the pastry, reserving a teaspoon for the glaze.
- Sprinkle the walnuts on top of the jam.
- Roll the dough up lengthwise using the plastic sheet to help.
- Using an oiled knife, cut the scrolls in thick slices.

Baking

- Preheat the oven to 180°C (350°F).
- Place scrolls on the baking tray and leave to rise for 20 minutes.
- Bake for 15 minutes.
- Remove from oven and glaze while hot.

Bun Glaze

- Boil ingredients together and brush on to hot buns.

Yeast-free Easter Ring

One medium-sized potato produces approximately 60g (2oz) mashed potato. Free of wheat, gluten, yeast, dairy and oil.

Ingredients

200mL (7fl oz) cold water
1 tsp salt
100g (4oz) caster (superfine) sugar
1 tbsp gelatine
60g (2oz) mashed potato
300g (10½oz) Lola's superfine flour
   (page 7)
1 tbsp ground ginger
1 tbsp mixed spice
1 tsp ground cinnamon
1 tbsp gluten-free baking powder
2 eggs
1 cup sultanas
1 apple, chopped

Preparation

- Place the cold water into a large glass bowl or microwave dish.
- Add the salt, caster sugar and gelatine.
- Let stand for 1 minute to soften.
- Grease a ring pan with some dairy-free margarine.
- Heat the gelatine mixture in the microwave for 50 seconds.

Mixing

- Whisk the mashed potato into the warm gelatine mixture.
- Combine the flour, spices and baking powder and dry whisk to blend.
- Whisk the eggs in a separate bowl with an electric mixer.
- Tip the dry ingredients into the potato mixture.
- Beat in the whisked eggs for 1 minute with electric mixer.

Baking

- Preheat the oven to 180°C (350°F).
- Pour a quarter of the mixture into the pan and spread over the base.
- Sprinkle a quarter of the sultanas and apple over the mixture and top with more mixture.
- Sprinkle over the remaining fruit and cover with more bun mixture.
- Leave to stand for 10 minutes.
- Place in the centre of the oven and bake 30 minutes.
- Remove from the oven, cover and cool in the tin.

For a festive appearance

- Ice with 2 cups pure icing (confectioners') sugar and 3 tablespoons margarine creamed together with a little hot water.
- Sprinkle with walnuts, cherries and citrus peel

Breakfast and Brunch

Amaranth Porridge

Amaranth cereal is made from the flowerets of a broad-leafed plant from South America. A centuries-old herb used by Aztecs and American Indians, it is higher in protein than wheat, corn or soya beans. According to the statistics on the packaging it is high in dietary fibre, as well as vitamins, calcium and many minerals. Apart from this it actually tastes good with a mild nutty flavour so is an ideal cereal for children as well as adults.

Ingredients

375mL (13fl oz) cold water
½ tsp salt
1 cup amaranth breakfast cereal
125mL (4fl oz) milk

Preparation

- Place the cold water and salt in a saucepan and bring to the boil.
- While stirring the water add the amaranth cereal in a steady stream.
- Cook for about 2 minutes,
- Add the milk, stir and cook until smooth.
- Serve hot with stewed prunes.

Poha Porridge

Poha is a fine-rolled rice flake thicker than baby rice cereal but thinner than the traditional hard-rolled rice flakes. The poha cooks quickly for an easy morning porridge. It is available from health food stores or Indian food shops.

Ingredients

375mL (13fl oz) cold water
1 tsp psyllium
pinch salt
½ cup rolled poha flakes
125mL (4fl oz) milk

Preparation

- In a small bowl place ½ cup cold water and the teaspoon of psyllium.
- Let stand about 2 minutes.
- Place 1 cup of water and the salt in a saucepan and bring to the boil.
- While stirring the water add the poha flakes in a steady stream.
- Cook for about 2 minutes, add the psyllium mixture and milk.
- Stir and cook until smooth.
- Serve hot with milk and brown sugar.

Dairy-free Hotcakes

Free of corn, wheat, soy, gluten and dairy, I use crumpet rings
to regulate the size of the hotcakes as they are a thin batter.
If you don't have crumpet rings use a small omelette pan.

Ingredients

2 eggs
65mL (2¼fl oz) (2fl oz) lemonade or
   soda water
2 tsp vanilla essence
2 tbsp olive oil
100g (4oz) Lola's superfine flour
   (page 7)
30g (1oz) caster (superfine) sugar
2 tsp gluten-free baking powder
½ cup extra oil to grease crumpet
   rings

Preparation

- Grease a flat pan or skillet with a little olive oil

Mixing

- Separate the eggs, put the two yolks in a medium-sized mixing bowl and retain the whites to beat separately.
- Add the lemonade, vanilla essence and oil to the egg yolks.
- Combine the flour, caster sugar and baking powder and whisk in the liquids using a wire whisk.
- Set aside.
- Whisk the two egg whites with a rotary or electric beater until stiff.
- Stir the stiffened egg into the hotcake batter and whisk well.
- Pour into a jug for easier handling while cooking.

Cooking

- Place some oil in a small pie tin to oil the crumpet rings.
- Heat the pan on medium heat.
- Pour about half a cupful of batter into crumpet rings in the greased pan.
- Let cook until the batter is set.
- Turn once to cook other side.
- Serve warm with honey or syrup.
- These hotcakes freeze well in a plastic container or in foil wrapped.

Bacon and Egg Waffles

Free of corn, wheat, soy and gluten.
You will need an electric waffle iron to cook the waffles.

Ingredients

1 cup milk
160g (5½oz) Lola's superfine flour
   (page 7)
1 tsp gluten-free baking powder
65mL (2¼fl oz) olive oil
1 tsp chopped parsley
pepper and salt to taste
2 rashers bacon or ham
2 eggs

Preparation

- Brush the waffle iron with oil and heat to manufacturer's instructions.
- Place the milk into a bowl and sift in the flour and baking powder.
- Mix with a whisk to ensure a smooth batter. Add the oil, parsley, salt and pepper.
- Remove the rind and chop the bacon or ham into small pieces, and add to the batter.
- Beat the eggs until light and fluffy and stir into the mixture.
- The batter should be very thin so that it will quickly and easily cover the waffle iron.
- Stir each time before pouring into waffle iron to distribute the bacon pieces.

Cooking

- Cook to waffle manufacturer's instructions.
- These waffles freeze well wrapped in foil.

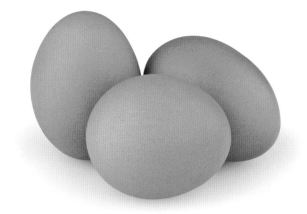

Breakfast on the Run

Free of corn, wheat, soy and gluten.
You will need an electric waffle iron to cook the waffles.

Ingredients

1 cup rolled rice flakes
1 tbsp psyllium
½ cup chopped dried apricots
2 cups water
1 tbsp gluten-free baking powder
160g (5½oz) Lola's superfine flour
  (page 7)
1 cup puffed amaranth cereal
½ cup desiccated coconut
½ cup chopped cashew nuts
65g (2¼oz) ground sunflower kernels
1 cup sultanas
2 tbsp honey
125g (4½oz) brown sugar
65mL (2¼fl oz) olive oil
1 beatten egg

Preparation

- Place the rice flakes, psyllium, apricots and water in a covered microwave dish and cook for 3 minutes in the microwave oven.

Mixing

- Add remaining ingredients to the cooked rice flake and apricot mixture.
- Stir well to combine ingredients and press into a 18 x 26 x 3cm deep.

Baking

- Preheat the oven to 160°C (320°F).
- Bake for 20 minutes.
- Remove from oven, cut into bars, separate and place on a baking tray.
- Return to oven and cook for a further 20 minutes.
- Let cool on the tray.
- Wrap and refrigerate until required.

Dairy-free Frittata

You can use leftover vegetables for this dish.

Ingredients

3 or 4 large mushrooms
1 brown-skinned potato,
unpeeled and sliced
½ cup cooked peas or beans

Basic Sauce

1 cup boiling water
2 sauce blocks
salt and pepper
3 beaten eggs or replacer

Sauce Blocks Ingredients

150g (5oz) dairy-free margarine
150g (5oz) Lola's superfine flour
   (page 7)

Preparation

- Make the basic sauce. Place the water in the saucepan, add the sauce blocks and let stand until soft. Return to the heat and whisk until it thickens.
- Season with salt and pepper.
- Remove from the heat and add the beaten eggs or replacer. Stand aside.
- Steam the sliced potatoes until tender.

Cooking

- In a frying pan sauté the mushrooms in a small amount of dairy-free margarine
- Add the sliced potatoes and beans, and fry for a few minutes to brown the potato.
- Pour the sauce mixture over the vegetables, reduce the heat and cook for about five minutes.
- Place the pan under a hot grill for 10 minutes to set the egg mixture.
- Serve immediately when cooked.

Sauce Blocks

I created these sauce blocks many years ago to simplify my cookery lessons. They are particularly useful in wheat-free cookery for sauces and gravy.

Preparation

- Melt the margarine in a saucepan over a low heat until it is soft.
- Remove from heat. Sift the flour into the softened margarine and return to the heat.
- Stir with a wooden spoon until the mixture will slide in the saucepan.
- Remove from the heat and set aside to cool slightly.
- Press the mixture into an ice-cube tray and freeze until required.

Date and Ginger Breakfast Bars

Yields four large 80g (3¾oz) bars. These great breakfast bars are ideal for snacks and take-out lunches. They will keep for at least two weeks in the refrigerator.

Ingredients

½ cup wholemeal rolled rice flakes
pinch salt
200mL (7fl oz) cold water
2 tbsp rice or maple syrup
1 tbsp sugar-free apricot jam
1 tsp almond essence
1 cup chopped dates
50g (2oz) desiccated coconut
50g (2oz) shredded coconut
50g (2oz) chopped chrystalised
    ginger
50g (2oz) ground almonds
2 tbsp rice flour
1 tbsp psyllium

Preparation

- Line a 22 x 8cm (8½ x 3¼in) slice tin with baking paper.
- Preheat the oven to 150°C (300°F).

Mixing

- Place the rice flakes, salt and cold water into a deep microwave dish.
- Cover and microwave on high for 3 minutes.
- Let stand for 3 minutes.
- Add the rice flake mixture to other ingredients.
- Mix well and press into the prepared tin.

Baking

- Bake for 20 minutes.
- Remove from the oven and cut the mixture into four bars.
- Place the cut bars back into the oven on a flat tray and bake for a further 20 minutes, turning once.
- Let cool before wrapping.

French Toast

You will need two slices of my sandwich bread or any gluten-free bread for this recipe.

Ingredients

1 egg
¼ cup milk
2 slices bread

Savoury Toast

salt and pepper

Sweet Toast

1 tbsp sugar
1 tsp vanilla essence
½ tsp ground cinnamon

Preparation

- Whisk together the egg and milk.
- For savoury toast, add salt and pepper to the mixture and whisk well.
- For sweet toast, add sugar, vanilla essence and cinnamon to the mixture and whisk well.

Cooking

- Melt a nob of butter in a frying pan.
- Dip the bread slices in the egg mixture, covering both sides.
- Place in the heated pan and cook for a few minutes both sides over medium heat.
- Serve with your favourite breakfast spread.

High-fibre Muesli Porridge

Makes one large or two small serves.

Ingredients

½ cup wholemeal rolled rice flakes
salt to taste
1 tsp psyllium
1 tsp ground almonds
1 tsp fine rice flour
1 tbsp sultanas
1 tbsp shredded coconut
1 cup cold water

Preparation

- Combine all the ingredients in a deep microwave bowl.
- Cover and microwave for 3 minutes.
- Serve with milk and brown sugar.

Fried Scones

These were a breakfast favourite of my grandfather. He loved them with golden syrup.

Ingredients

30g (1oz) margarine
125mL (4fl oz) cold water
1 tsp salt
2 tsp gluten-free baking powder
100g (4oz) Lola's superfine flour
   (page 7)
65mL (2¼fl oz) olive oil

Mixing

- Chop the margarine into tiny cubes.
- Place the cold water into a small mixing bowl.
- Add the margarine, salt, baking powder and flour.
- Mix to a soft dough, press out and cut into squares.

Cooking

- Place the oil in a frying pan and heat to a medium heat.
- Carefully place the scones into the heated oil and cook until golden.
- Turn over and cook the other side for a few minutes until firm.
- Serve warm with golden syrup.

Polenta Porridge

Ingredients

1 cup boiling water
salt to taste
½ cup fine polenta (cornmeal)
½ cup milk

Preparation

- Place the boiling water in a saucepan on high heat and boil rapidly.
- While briskly stirring the water with a wooden spoon, trickle the polenta into the saucepan in a fine steady stream.
- Continue stirring until it is thick and cooked, about 2 minutes.
- Stir in the milk and serve hot with yoghurt or creamy milk.
- Season with salt as desired.

Potato Cakes

Chopped bacon or ham can be added for extra flavour.

Ingredients

1 egg
1 potato, unpeeled and coarsely grated
2 tbsp Lola's superfine flour (page 7)
salt and pepper

Preparation

- Lightly whisk the egg and add to the grated potato.
- Fold in the flour, salt and pepper.

Cooking

- Heat a small amount of oil in a shallow pan.
- Fry over a medium heat until golden, turn once
- Serve with baked beans, sautéed mushrooms or tomatoes..

Thai Porridge

This porridge is called 'Frogs Eggs' by children and is served with yoghurt, chopped cashew nuts and honey. For added nutrition, a whisked egg can be added to the final stage of cooking.

Ingredients

½ cup large tapioca soaked in 1 cup boiling water overnight
1 cup milk (skim, full cream or rice)
1 tbsp sugar
1 tbsp shredded coconut

Preparation

- Place the soaked tapioca in a saucepan over high heat.
- Add milk, stirring constantly until it boils.
- Reduce the heat and simmer for 20 minutes.
- Add the sugar and shredded coconut to the porridge.
- A whisked egg can be added here for extra nutrition.
- Cook gently for one more minute.
- Serve warm with yoghurt, honey and chopped cashew nuts.

These methods are suitable for cafes, hospitals, nursing homes and institutions—where gluten-free products are required and preparation time is important.

These recipes use my Bread improver, which is available by mail (see wheatfree world.com.au). Or you can use a substitute of 2 tablespoons of dried egg white plus 1 teaspoon of citric acid.

This allows the mixes to be prepacked, ready for mixing with just the addition of water and oil.

English Muffins

These muffins are cooked in Yorkshire pudding tins but can be cooked in large muffin tins. A flat top is achieved by placing a scone tray on top of the rising loaf 10 minutes into the baking time.

Ingredients

500mL (17½fl oz) warm water
65mL (2¼fl oz) olive oil
1 tbsp glycerine
2 tbsp gelatine
2 tbsp Lola's bread improver
2 tsp salt
2 tsp sugar
2 tbsp dried yeast
500g (17½oz) Lola's superfine flour
  (page 7)
1 tbsp mixed spice
1 cup mixed fruit
1 apple, finely chopped

Preparation

- Grease the Yorkshire pudding trays with margarine.
- Place the water, oil and glycerine into large mixing bowl.

Mixing

- Add the dry ingredients to the liquids and mix well for about 1 minute.
- Cover the bowl with a large plastic bag; no need to remove the beater.
- Leave to rise for 10–15 minutes.
- Beat the mixture for 1 minute.
- Fold in the fruit and spoon into greased trays.
- Preheat the oven to 200°C (400°F).
- Leave the mixture to rise for 20 minutes or less until it is puffy.

Baking

- Bake on the middle shelf for 25 minutes.
- Remove from oven and wrap in a clean tea towel.

Everyday Breads

Bacon Bread Ring

Use a 20cm (7¾in) ring tin.
Low-fat option: The bacon pieces can be grilled to remove fat
if desired or you can add them raw and decrease the oil to
2 tablespoons, plus 2 tablespoons of warm water.

Ingredients

1 cup cold water
1 tsp salt
1 tsp sugar
2 tsp psyllium
2 tsp gelatine
1 tbsp dried yeast
1 egg white
½ tsp citric acid
65mL (2¼fl oz) olive oil
250g (8½oz) Lola's superfine flour
  (page 7)
100g (4oz) bacon pieces

Preparation

- Place the cold water in a large glass bowl or microwave dish.
- Add the salt, sugar, psyllium and gelatine.
- Let stand for 1 minute to soften gelatine.
- Heat the mixture in the microwave on high for 40 seconds.
- Grease a ring pan with margarine.

Mixing

- Remove the mixture from microwave.
- Stir in the yeast and whisk slightly. Let stand for 10 minutes.
- Beat the egg white and citric acid until stiff, and add to yeast mixture with the oil and flour.
- Using an electric mixer beat well for about 2 minutes.
- Cover and let rise for 10 minutes. Whisk for 1 minute.
- Fold in the chopped bacon pieces.
- Spoon into the prepared baking pan, cover and leave again for 20 minutes to rise.

Baking

- While the mixture is standing, preheat the oven to 180°C (350°F).
- Place pan in the centre of the oven and bake for 40 minutes.
- Remove from the oven and wrap in a clean tea towel to cool.

Brown Fruit Loaf

This bread is not too sweet, can be eaten warm and is good for lunches. Note: The grainy texture is achieved by the blending of sunflower kernels to a meal. Loaf tin 28 x 12 x 10cm (11 x 4¾ x 4in) deep.

Ingredients

450g (16oz) Lola's supefine flour (page 7)
1 tsp carob or cocoa
50g (2oz) sunflower meal
2 cups cold water
2 tsp salt
1 tbsp treacle
2 tbsp gelatine
100g (4oz) pitted prunes
2 tbsp dried yeast
3 egg whites
2 tbsp caster (superfine) sugar
1 tsp citric acid
65mL (2¼fl oz) olive oil

Preparation

- Grease the tin well with margarine.
- Combine the flour, carob and sunflower meal in a plastic bag and shake well.
- Place the cold water, salt, treacle and gelatine in large mixing bowl. Stand for 2 minutes.
- Chop the prunes in small pieces, dust with a little of the flour to separate.

Mixing

- Heat the gelatine mixture in the microwave for 1 minute.
- Add the flour mixture and yeast to the gelatine mixture and mix well for about 1 minute in an electric mixing machine.
- Cover the bowl with a large plastic bag; no need to remove the beater.
- Leave to rise for 10–15 minutes.
- Preheat the oven to 180°C (350°F).
- Beat the egg whites in a separate bowl with the caster sugar and citric acid until stiff.
- Add the beaten egg whites and oil to the bread mixture.
- Beat the mixture for 2 minutes and pour a thin layer into the prepared tin to coat the bottom of the tin and prevent the fruit sticking to the bottom.
- Sprinkle the chopped prunes over the batter and add the remaining mixture.
- Leave to rise for 30 minutes or less until the mixture is 2½cm (1in) from the top of the tin.

Baking

- Bake on lower shelf for 1 hour.
- Remove from oven and wrap in a clean tea towel to cool.

Poppy Seed Plaits

I use a four-loaf plait tin for this recipe. One medium-sized potato produces approximately 60g (2oz) mashed potato.

Ingredients

1 tbsp gelatine
2 tsp salt
2 tsp sugar
400mL (14fl oz) cold water
120g (4oz) warm mashed potato
125mL (4fl oz) olive oil
2 tbsp dried yeast
500g (17½oz) Lola's superfine flour
   (page 7)
2 egss
3 tbsp poppy seeds
1 tbsp extra poppy seeds for the tin

Preparation

- Place the gelatine, salt and sugar in the cold water and let stand for 2 minutes.
- Preheat the oven to 200°C (400°F).
- Grease the bread tins well with margarine.
- Line with the extra poppy seeds.

Mixing

- When the gelatine has softened heat the mixture until clear.
- Tip the hot gelatine mixture into the mashed potato and mix well.
- Add the olive oil to this mixture and while it is still warm add the yeast.
- Sift in the flour.
- Beat the eggs and add to the mixture.
- Beat the mixture with an electric beater for about 1 minute. (The mixture should be a thick batter. Add a little more warm water if too stiff.)
- Fold the seeds into the mixture and pour the batter into the prepared tin.
- Let it stand for 10–15 minutes or until mixture is 'puffy'. It will continue to rise in the oven.

Baking

- Cook for about 20 minutes or until the loaves sound hollow when tapped.

Small White Loaf

Note: There is no oil in this loaf so it doesn't freeze for long.
It is baked in a tin 18 x 11 x 10cm (7 x 4 x 4in) deep.

Ingredients

125mL (4fl oz) boiling water
125mL (4fl oz) cold water
1 tbsp dried yeast
1 tbsp sugar
1 tbsp gelatine
1 tsp salt
½ tsp citric acid
1 tbsp psyllium
300g (10½oz) Lola's superfine flour
    (page 7)
2 egg whites

Preparation

- Grease a bread tin with margarine to hold the paper in place. Line with baking paper.
- Place the water, hot and cold, into a medium-sized glass or plastic bowl.
- Add the yeast, sugar, gelatine, salt and psyllium.
- Lightly whisk to mix ingredients.
- Cover the bowl and leave to rise for 15 minutes.

Mixing

- Add the flour, citric acid and egg whites to the yeast mixture and mix for 2 minutes, using an electric beater.
- Cover the bowl with a large plastic bag and leave to rise for 20 minutes.
- Beat the mixture for 1 minute and scrape into a prepared tin.
- Preheat oven to 220°C (420°F).
- Cover the tin with the plastic bag and leave to rise for 25 minutes or less until the mixture is 2cm from the top of the tin.

Baking

- Bake on the lower shelf for 40 minutes.
- Remove from oven and wrap in a clean tea towel.
- Do not cut until cool.

Crusty Shell Loaf

This loaf is baked in a shell-shaped steel mould. It can be used as a centrepiece for a buffet—simply slice the loaf through to form a lid and fill it with salad and seafood such seafood extender or crabsticks.

Ingredients

1 tsp salt
1 tsp sugar
1 tbsp dried yeast
1 cup warm water
250g (8½oz) Lola's superfine flour
  (page 7)
1 egg white
sesame seeds for garnish

Preparation

- Add the salt, sugar and yeast to warm water and let stand for 10 minutes.
- Grease a small bread tin with margarine and line it with seeds or baking paper.
- Preheat oven to 200°C (400°F).

Mixing

- Add the flour to the yeast mixture, and beat for 1 minute with electric mixer.
- Cover and leave to rise until 'puffy' about 10 minutes.
- Beat the egg white.
- Add to the mixture and beat again for 1 minute.
- Pour into prepared tin and let stand for another 10 minutes to rise.
- Sprinkle with seeds or grated cheese if preferred.

Baking

- Bake for 15 minutes.

Hi-top Grain Loaf

The grainy texture is achieved by the addition of sunflower
meal made by blending sunflower kernels for a few minutes.
Use a heavy bread tin 28 x 12 x 10cm (11 x4¾ x4in) deep.

Ingredients

2 cups cold water
2 tbsp gelatine
2 tsp sugar
2 tsp salt
450g (16oz) Lola's superfine flour
  (page 7)
60g (2oz) brown rice flour
2 tbsp dried yeast
3 egg whites
60g (2oz) sunflower meal
65mL (2¼fl oz) olive oil

Preparation

- Grease a bread tin with margarine to hold the paper in place. Line with baking paper.
- Place the cold water into large mixing bowl add the gelatine, sugar and salt.
- Stand for 2 minutes to soften the gelatine.

Mixing

- Heat the gelatine mixture for approximately 1 minute until clear.
- Add the flour, rice flour and yeast to the warm liquid and beat with an electric mixer for about 1 minute.
- Cover the bowl with a large plastic bag; no need to remove the beater.
- Leave to rise for 10 minutes.
- Whisk the egg whites in a separate bowl until stiff.
- Add the beaten egg whites, sunflower meal and oil to the bread mixture and beat for about 2 minutes.
- Preheat the oven to 200°C (400°F).
- Pour the mixture into the prepared tin and leave to rise for 20–25 minutes until about 2½cm (1in) from the top of the tin.

Baking

- Bake on the lowest shelf of the oven for 1 hour.
- Remove from oven and wrap in a clean tea towel.
- Do not cut until cold.

This loaf freezes well; it is better to slice it before freezing.
An electric knife is very good for slicing gluten-free bread.

Hamburger Buns

This recipe makes 12 large buns. I use three heavy Yorkshire pudding trays but they can also be made in muffin or pie tins. These buns freeze well.

Ingredients

2 cups cold water
2 tbsp gelatine
2 tsp sugar
2 tsp salt
500g (17½oz) Lola's superfine flour (page 7)
2 tbsp dried yeast
3 egg whites
½ tsp citric acid
65mL (2¼fl oz) olive oil

Preparation

- Grease the trays with margarine.
- Place the cold water into a large mixing bowl and add the gelatine, sugar and salt.
- Stand for 2 minutes to soften the gelatine.

Mixing

- Heat the gelatine mixture for approximately 1 minute until clear.
- Add the flour and yeast to the warm liquid and beat with an electric mixer for about 1 minute.
- Cover the bowl with a large plastic bag; no need to remove the beater.
- Leave to rise for 10 minutes.
- Whisk the egg whites and citric acid in a separate bowl until stiff.
- Add the beaten egg whites and oil to the bread mixture and beat for about 2 minutes.
- Preheat the oven to 200°C (400°F).
- Pour the mixture into the prepared pans and leave to rise for 10–15 minutes until they are 'puffy'.

Baking

- Bake on the middle shelf of the oven for 15 minutes.
- Remove from oven and wrap in a clean tea towel.
- Do not cut until cold.

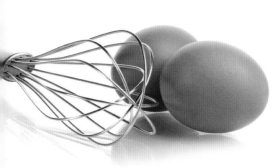

Herb and Onion Bread

I use a ribbed-bottom 30 x 8cm (11¾ x 3¼in)
saddle tin to cook this small loaf.

Ingredients

1 tbsp gelatine
1 tsp sugar
1 tsp salt
200mL (7fl oz) cold water
1 tbsp sesame seeds
1 tbsp dried yeast
250g (8½oz) Lola's superfine flour
   (page 7)
1 egg
65mL (2¼fl oz) olive oil
1 tbsp dried onion
1 tsp fresh or dried herbs

Preparation

- Place the gelatine, sugar and salt into the cold water and let stand for about 2 minutes to soften the gelatine.
- Preheat the oven to 200°C (400°F) .
- Select a 30 x 8cm (11¾ x 3in) saddle tin to cook the loaf.
- Grease the tin well with margarine and sprinkle with sesame seeds.

Mixing

- When the gelatine has softened heat the mixture for 30 seconds and add the yeast.
- Stand for 10 minutes to 'puff' the yeast.
- Sift in the flour.
- Add the egg and oil and beat the mixture with an electric beater for about 1 minute. (The mixture should be a thick batter. Add a little more warm water if too stiff.)
- Fold in the dried onion and herbs and pour into the prepared tin.
- Leave the mixture to rise in the tin for 10–15 minutes, or until mixture is 1¼cm (½in) from top of tin.
- It will continue to rise in the oven.

Baking

- Cook for about 40 minutes or until the loaf sounds hollow when tapped.

Butternut Bread

I use a ribbed bottom 30 x 8cm (11¾ x 3in) saddle tin to cook this small loaf. Note: This loaf was baked using 2 egg yolks, which can be replaced with 1 egg or equivalent egg replacer.

Ingredients

1 tbsp gelatine
1 tsp sugar
1 tsp salt
200mL (7fl oz) cold water
pumpkin seeds
1 tbsp dried yeast
250g (8½oz) Lola's superfine flour
    (page 7)
2 egg yolks
65mL (2¼fl oz) olive oil
60g (2oz) grated butternut pumpkin

Preparation

- Place the gelatine, sugar and salt into the cold water and let stand for about 2 minutes to soften the gelatine.
- Preheat the oven to 200°C (400°F).
- Grease the loaf tin well with margarine and sprinkle with seeds from the pumpkin.

Mixing

- When the gelatine has softened heat the mixture for 1 minute and while it is still warm add the yeast.
- Stand for 10 minutes to 'puff' the yeast.
- Sift in the flour and egg or egg-replacer mixture.
- Add the oil and beat the mixture with an electric beater for about 1 minute. (The mixture should be a thick batter. Add a little more warm water if too stiff.)
- Pour a thin layer of the batter into the prepared tin and sprinkle about one third of the grated pumpkin over it.
- Repeat the method until all the batter and pumpkin is used.
- Leave the mixture to rise in the tin for 10–15 minutes, or until mixture is 1¼cm (½in) from top of tin. It will still continue to rise in the oven.

Baking

- Cook for about 40 minutes or until the loaf sounds hollow when tapped.

High-fibre Yeast-free Loaf

I use a 28 x 12 x 10cm (11 x 4¾ x 4in) loaf tin.

Ingredients

2 cups cold water
1 tbsp gelatine
2 tbsp psyllium
500g (17½oz) Lola's superfine flour
  (page 7)
3 tbsp gluten-free baking powder
3 egg whites
2 tsp salt
1 tsp sugar
2 tbsp olive oil

Preparation

- Place 1 cup cold water in a small bowl and sprinkle the gelatine over it. Let stand until the gelatine sinks, then heat the mixture in the microwave for 20 seconds on high.
- Place remaining cold water into small bowl and sprinkle the psyllium on top; whisk in.
- Leave to stand about for 2 minutes until the mixture is thick.
- Grease a large bread tin and line it with baking paper.
- Combine the flour and baking powder.

Mixing

- Beat the egg whites, salt and sugar until stiff.
- Spoon the warm gelatine mixture into the egg whites, a little at a time while beating; it should end up like meringue.
- Fold the psyllium mixture into the beaten egg whites.
- Add oil and dry ingredients and beat for 1 minute with an electric mixer.
- Pour mixture into the prepared bread tin and let stand for 10 minutes.

Baking

- While the mixture is standing, preheat the oven to 200°C (400°F) .
- Cook loaf in the centre of the oven for 50–60 minutes.
- Remove from the tin and wrap in a damp cloth until cold.

Linseed and Cheese Loaf

I use a heavy 28 x 12 x 10cm (11 x 4¾ x 4in) bread tin to bake this loaf.

Ingredients

2 tbsp gelatine
375mL (13fl oz) cold water
65mL (2¼fl oz) olive oil
1 tsp sugar
1 tsp salt
2 tbsp dried yeast
500g (17½oz) Lola's superfine flour (page 7)
20g (²/₃oz) baby rice flake cereal
2 eggs
50g (2oz) linseeds
100g (4oz) grated tasty cheese

Preparation

- Place the gelatine in the cold water and let stand to soften.
- Preheat the oven to 200°C (400°F) .
- Grease the tin well with margarine. Line with extra linseeds if desired.

Mixing

- When the gelatine has softened heat the mixture until clear.
- Add the olive oil, sugar and salt to this mixture and while it is still warm add the yeast.
- Sift in the flour and baby rice flake cereal.
- Beat the eggs and add to the mixture.
- Beat with an electric beater for about 1 minute. (The mixture should be a thick batter. Add a little more warm water if too stiff.)
- Fold in the grated cheese and linseeds and pour the batter into the prepared tin.
- Let it stand for 15 minutes, or until mixture is 1¼cm from top of tin.
- It will continue to rise in the oven.

Baking

- Cook for about 50 minutes or until the loaf sounds hollow when tapped.

Seeded Country Loaf

This loaf is baked in a tin 18 x 11 x 8cm (7 x 4 x 3in) deep. Blending sunflower kernels for about 1 minute makes sunflower meal.

Ingredients

65mL (2¼fl oz) cold water
1 tsp gelatine
125mL (4fl oz) warm water
1 tsp sugar
1 tbsp glycerine
1 tbsp parisian essence
1 tbsp dried yeast
250g (8½oz) Lola's superfine flour
   (page 7)
30g (1oz) sunflower meal
2 egg whites
1 tsp salt
2 tbsp olive oil
3 tbsp mixed seeds such as linseed,
   sesame or poppy

Preparation

- Place the cold water in a small bowl and sprinkle the gelatine over it.
- Let stand for 1 minute, then heat for 30 seconds on high in microwave.
- Grease a loaf pan and line with baking paper.
- Place the warm water in a bowl with sugar, glycerine, Parisian essence and yeast.
- Whisk lightly and let stand until frothy; 10–15 minutes.
- Combine the flour and sunflower meal.

Mixing

- Beat the egg whites and salt until stiff.
- Spoon the warm gelatine mixture into the egg whites while beating, a little at a time.
- Pour the frothy yeast mixture into the eggs; fold in the dry ingredients with a large wire whisk.
- Cover and let stand for 20 minutes.
- Add the oil and whisk again with an electric mixer for 1 minute.
- Fold in seeds and pour into the bread tin. Cover and leave to rise for 30 minutes.

Baking

- While the mixture is rising, preheat the oven to 200°C (400°F).
- Place tin on the middle shelf and bake for 40 minutes.
- Remove from the tin, wrap in a clean tea towel and leave to cool before cutting.

Damper

Ingredients

65mL (2¼fl oz) cold water
1 tbsp psyllium
1 egg
2 tsp milk or water for egg wash
65mL (2¼fl oz) warm water
200g (7oz) Lola's superfine flour
   (page 7)
2 tbsp milk powder
1 tbsp gluten-free baking powder
1 tsp salt

Preparation

- Preheat oven to 220°C (420°F).
- Grease an oven tray or cover with baking paper.
- Place the cold water in a small bowl and sprinkle the psyllium on top.
- Whisk lightly and leave to gel for about 3 minutes.

Egg Wash

- To make egg wash without using an additional egg: lightly whisk the egg in a small mixing bowl.
- Tip the egg into a large mixing bowl to use in the damper mixture, then add 2 teaspoons of milk or water to the small bowl.
- Wash around the bowl with the pastry brush and you have egg wash to glaze the damper.

Mixing

- To the egg used to make the wash add the warm water and psyllium mix.
- Place the flour, milk powder, baking powder and salt in a plastic bag and shake well. Add three quarters of the flour mixture to the egg mixture and fold with a table knife to combine into a soft dough. Do not mix more than necessary.
- Place the remaining flour mixture on a board in a well shape.
- Tip the soft dough into the well.
- Knead very quickly a few times to combine all the ingredients.
- Shape into a damper and mark sections with a knife.

Baking

- Place on the baking tray and glaze with the egg wash.
- Cook on a high shelf in the oven for about 15 minutes.
- Remove from the oven and cool on a wire rack covered with a damp tea towel.

Yeast-free Saddle Loaf

Use a 30cm (11¾in) saddle tin. This mixture is also good for yeast-free burger buns or a focaccia if cooked in a slab tin.

Ingredients

65mL (2¼fl oz) cold water
1 tsp gelatine
125mL (4fl oz) warm water
1 tbsp glycerine
250g (8½oz) Lola's superfine flour (page 7)
3 tsp gluten-free baking powder
2 egg whites
½ tsp salt
2 tbsp extra warm water
1 tbsp olive oil

Preparation

- Place the cold water in a small bowl and sprinkle the gelatine over it. Let stand until the gelatine sinks.
- Heat the mixture in the microwave for 20 seconds on high.
- Grease the bread tin and line it with baking paper or sprinkle with seeds.
- Place the warm water into a small bowl with the glycerine.
- Place the flour and baking powder into a large bowl and blend with a wire whisk to distribute the baking powder.

Mixing

- Beat the egg whites and salt until stiff. Spoon the warm gelatine mixture into the egg whites while beating, a little at a time.
- Pour the warm glycerine mixture into the beaten egg whites, add the dry ingredients and fold the mixture with a large wire whisk.
- Whisk again and add the oil and the extra 2 tablespoons of warm water.
- Check the consistency; it should pour like custard, add more water if necessary.
- Pour into the prepared bread tin and cover with plastic wrap.
- Let stand for 10 minutes.

Baking

- While the mixture is standing, preheat oven to 200°C (400°F) .
- Cook loaf in the centre of the oven for 40 minutes.
- Remove from the tin and wrap in a damp cloth until cold.

Tall Milk Loaf

I make this loaf in a 16cm (6¼in) round high tin.

Ingredients

1 cup cold water
1 tsp salt
1 tsp sugar
2 tsp psyllium
2 tsp gelatine
1 tbsp dried yeast
250g (8½oz) Lola's superfine flour
  (page 7)
½ tsp citric acid
60g (2oz) milk powder
1 egg
65mL (2¼fl oz) olive oil

Preparation

- Place the cold water in a large glass bowl or microwave dish.
- Add the salt, sugar, psyllium and gelatine.
- Let stand for 1 minute to soften gelatine.
- Heat the mixture in the microwave on high for 40 seconds.
- Grease a high pan with dairy-free margarine.

Mixing

- Remove the mixture from microwave.
- Stir in the yeast and whisk slightly. Let stand for 20 minutes.
- Combine flour, citric acid and milk powder.
- Tip the dry ingredients into the yeast mixture.
- Add the egg and oil and beat with an electric mixer for about 2 minutes.
- Cover and let rise for 20 minutes. Whisk for 1 minute.
- Spoon into the prepared baking pan, cover and leave again for 30 minutes.

Baking

- Preheat oven to 160°C (320°F).
- Place in the centre of the oven and bake for 1 hour.
- Remove from the oven and wrap in a clean tea towel to cool.
- Note: The lower oven temperature is necessary to prevent the loaf from over-browning caused by the milk powder.

White Sandwich Loaf

Use a heavy-duty loaf tin, 28 x 12 x 10cm (11 x 4¾ x 4in) deep. A flat top is achieved by placing a scone tray on top of the rising loaf 10 minutes into the baking time.

Ingredients

2 cups cold water
2 tbsp gelatine
2 tsp sugar
2 tsp salt
500g (17½oz) Lola's superfine flour
   (page 7)
2 tbsp dried yeast
3 egg whites
1 tsp citric acid
65mL (2¼fl oz) olive oil

Preparation

- Grease a bread tin with margarine to hold the paper in place. Line with baking paper.
- Place the cold water into large mixer bowl and add the gelatine, sugar and salt.
- Stand for 2 minutes to soften the gelatine.

Mixing

- Heat the gelatine mixture for approximately 1 minute until clear.
- Add the flour and yeast to the warm liquid and beat with electric mixer for about one minute.
- Cover the bowl with a large plastic bag; no need to remove the beater
- Leave to rise for 10 minutes.
- Whisk the egg whites and citric acid in a separate bowl until stiff.
- Add the beaten egg whites and oil to the bread mixture and beat for about 2 minutes with an electric mixer.
- Preheat the oven to 200°C (400°F) .
- Pour the mixture into the prepared tin and leave to rise for 20–25 minutes until about 2½cm (1in) from the top of the tin.

Baking

- Bake on the lowest shelf of the oven for 1 hour.
- Ten minutes after placing the bread in the oven, top with a piece of baking paper and a scone tray to give a flat top for sandwich making.
- Remove from oven and wrap in a clean tea towel.
- Do not cut until cold.
- This loaf freezes well; it is better to slice it before freezing.
- An electric knife is very good for slicing gluten-free bread.

Yeast-free Brown Loaf

The mixture for this loaf should be of butter cake consistency; 2 extra tablespoons of warm water may be needed as some sunflower seeds are drier than others. Blending sunflower kernels for about 1 minute makes sunflower meal.

Ingredients

65mL (2¼fl oz) cold water
1 tsp gelatine
125mL (4fl oz) warm water
1 tbsp glycerine
1 tbsp olive oil
1 tbsp parisian essence
200g (7oz) Lola's superfine flour
   (page 7)
3 tsp gluten-free baking powder
60g (2oz) sunflower meal
2 egg whites
1 tsp salt

Preparation

- Place the cold water in a small bowl and sprinkle the gelatine over it. Let stand until the gelatine sinks, then heat the mixture in the microwave for 20 seconds on high.
- Grease a loaf pan and line it with baking paper.
- Place the warm water into a small bowl with the glycerine, oil and Parisian essence.
- Place the flour, baking powder and sunflower meal into a large bowl and blend it with a wire whisk.

Mixing

- Beat the egg whites and salt until stiff.
- Spoon the warm gelatine mixture into the egg whites while beating, a little at a time.
- Pour the warm Parisian essence mixture into the beaten egg whites, add the dry ingredients and fold the mixture with a large wire whisk.
- Check the consistency; it should pour like custard, add the extra water if necessary.
- Pour into the prepared bread tin and cover with plastic wrap. Let stand for 10 minutes.

Baking

- While the mixture is standing, preheat the oven to 200°C (400°F).
- Cook in the centre of the oven for 40 minutes.
- Remove from the tin and wrap in a damp cloth until cold.

Basic Potato Bread

I use a ribbed-bottom 30 x 8cm (11¾ x 3¼in) saddle tin to cook this small loaf. Note: It is important to catch the rising yeast at just the right time, because if you leave it to rise too long it will collapse. One medium sized potato produces approximately 60g (2oz) mashed potato.

Ingredients

1 tbsp gelatine
200mL (7fl oz) cold water
65g warm mashed potato
65mL (2¼fl oz) olive oil
1 tsp sugar
1 tsp salt
1 tbsp dried yeast
250g (8½oz) Lola's superfine flour
  (page 7)
1 egg (egg replacer can be used in
  this recipe)

Preparation

- Place the gelatine in the cold water and let stand to soften.
- Preheat the oven to 200°C (400°F).
- Grease the loaf tin well with margarine.
- Line with seeds if desired.

Mixing

- When the gelatine has softened heat the mixture until clear.
- Tip the hot gelatine mixture into the mashed potato and mix well.
- Add the olive oil, sugar and salt to this mixture and while it is still warm add the yeast.
- Sift in the flour and the egg or egg-replacer mix.
- Beat the mixture with an electric beater for about 1 minute. (The mixture should be a thick batter; add a little more warm water if too stiff.)
- Pour the batter into the prepared tin and let it stand for 10–15 minutes, or until mixture is 1¼cm (½in) from top of tin.
- It will still continue to rise in the oven.

Baking

- Cook for about 40 minutes or until the loaf sounds hollow when tapped.

Note: This loaf can be doubled for a large bread tin. If you want a square loaf, place a greased scone tray on top of the bread tin, and allow another 10 minutes of cooking.

Large Grain Loaf

Use a heavy-duty loaf tin, 28 x 12 x 10cm (11 x 4¾ x 4in) deep.
The grainy texture is achieved by the addition of sunflower
meal and brown rice flour.

Ingredients

375mL (13fl oz) cold water
125mL (4fl oz) boiling water
65mL (2¼fl oz) olive oil
1 tbsp glycerine
2 tbsp gelatine
2 tsp salt
2 tsp sugar
450g (16oz) Lola's superfine flour
   (page 7)
60g (2oz) brown rice flour
60g (2oz) sunflower meal
2 tbsp dried yeast
2 tbsp Lola's bread improver

Preparation

- Grease a bread tin with margarine to hold the paper in place. Line with baking paper.
- Place all the liquids, hot and cold, oil and glycerine into large mixing bowl.

Mixing

- Add the dry ingredients to the liquids and mix well for about 1 minute.
- Cover the bowl with a large plastic bag; no need to remove the beater.
- Leave to rise for 10 minutes.
- Beat the mixture for 30 seconds, cover and let rise for another 10 minutes.
- Preheat the oven to 200°C (400°F).
- Beat the mixture for 30 seconds again and pour into the prepared tin.
- Cover with the plastic bag and leave to rise for 30 minutes or less until the mixture is 2½cm (1in) from the top of the tin.

Baking

- Bake on the lower shelf for 1 hour.
- Remove from oven and wrap in a clean tea towel.
- Do not cut until cool.

Sandwich Loaf

Use a heavy-duty loaf tin, 28 x 12 x 10cm deep (11 x 4¾ x 4in).
A flat top is achieved by placing a scone tray on top of the
rising loaf 10 minutes into the baking time.

Ingredients

2 cups warm water
2 tbsp gelatine
2 tsp salt
2 tsp sugar
2 tbsp dried yeast
1 tbsp glycerine
500g (17½oz) Lola's superfine flour
(page 7)
2 tbsp Lola's bread improver
65mL (2¼fl oz) olive oil

Preparation

- Grease a bread tin and line with baking paper.
- Place the warm water in a large mixing bowl.

Mixing

- Add the dry ingredients to the warm liquid and beat with an
  electric mixer for 1 minute.
- Cover the bowl with a large plastic bag; no need to remove
  the beater.
- Leave to rise for 10 minutes.
- Beat again for 2 minutes.
- Cover and stand for 10 minutes.
- Preheat the oven to 200°C (400°F).
- Beat in the oil and pour into the prepared tin.
- Leave to rise for about 20–25 minutes until about 2½cm from
  the top of the tin.

Baking

- Bake on the lowest shelf of the oven.
- Ten minutes after placing the bread in the oven, top with a
  piece of baking paper
  and a scone tray to give a flat top for sandwich-making.
- Bake for 1 hour.
- Remove from oven and wrap in a clean tea towel.
- Do not cut until cold.
- This loaf freezes well; it is better to slice it before freezing.
- An electric knife is very good for slicing gluten-free bread.

Around the World

Baps (Scotland)

These soft-topped rolls were baked in Yorkshire pudding trays; they are served fresh from the oven for breakfast in Scotland.

Ingredients

200mL (7fl oz) cold water
1 tsp sugar
1 tbsp gelatine
1 tbsp dried yeast
2 egg whites
1 tsp salt
½ tsp citric acid
250g (8½oz) Lola's superfine flour
    (page 7)
2 tbsp olive oil

Preparation

- Place the cold water into a large glass bowl or microwave dish.
- Add the sugar and gelatine.
- Let stand for 1 minute to soften.
- Grease a Yorkshire pudding tray with some dairy-free margarine.

Mixing

- Heat the gelatine mixture in the microwave for 50 seconds.
- Add the yeast and stand for 10 minutes.
- Whisk the eggs, salt and citric acid in a separate bowl with an electric mixer until stiff.
- Tip the flour into the yeast mixture.
- Beat in the oil and whisked eggs for 1 minute with electric mixer.
- Cover and let stand again for 10 minutes.

Baking

- Preheat the oven to 180°C (350°F).
- Spoon the mixture into the tins and leave until puffy; about 15 minutes.
- Dust the tops with sifted flour.
- Place in the centre of the oven and bake for 10 minutes.
- Remove from the oven and wrap in a clean tea towel to cool then place in a plastic bag until ready to serve.

Black Bread (Hungary)

This gluten-free version of traditional black bread is baked in a bowl-shaped tin that is lined with poppy seeds. Blending sunflower kernels for a few minutes in the blender makes sunflower meal.

Ingredients

1 tsp salt
¼ cup molasses
1 tbsp dried yeast
1 cup warm water
160g (5½oz) Lola's superfine flour (page 7)
80g sunflower meal
1 tbsp carob
1 tbsp psyllium
100g (4oz) brown rice flour
1 egg
65mL (2¼fl oz) olive oil
1 tsp parisian essence
1 tbsp caraway seeds
2 tbsp poppy seeds for lining tin

Preparation

- Add the salt, molasses and yeast to the warm water and stand 10 minutes.
- Grease a small bowl-shaped tin with some margarine and line it with poppy seeds, or line a ceramic flowerpot with aluminium foil.
- Combine the flour, sunflower meal, carob, psyllium and rice flour.

Mixing

- Add half the flour mixture to the yeast and whisk in the egg and oil then beat in the remaining flour and Parisian essence with an electric mixer.
- Cover and let stand again for 15 minutes.

Baking

- Preheat the oven to 180°C (350°F).
- Whisk the bread mixture, add the caraway seeds, pour into the seeded tin and leave to rise for about 20 minutes.
- Remove from the oven and cool in the tin.
- Wrap in a clean tea towel and refrigerate overnight before cutting.

Tip: If you measure the oil first and then measure the molasses in the same oily measure cup, the molasses will easily slide from the cup.

Challah Plait (Israel)

Pronounced (Hallah) this plaited soft bread with a golden colour and seeded top is used as Friday night bread by the Jewish community. For New Year it is baked with sultanas in round loaves (to represent the roundness of the year). At the evening meal it is customary to eat symbolic foods. Bake it in a plait-patterned or ring tin.

Ingredients

2 cups cold water
1 tbsp gelatine
3 tbsp sesame seeds
2 tbsp dried yeast
3egg whites
2 tbsp sugar
2 tsp salt
1 tsp citric acid
500g (17½oz) Lola's superfine flour
   (page 7)
3 tbsp olive oil

Preparation

- Place the cold water into a large glass bowl or microwave dish.
- Add gelatine and let stand for 1 minute to soften.
- Grease a plait-patterned or ring tin with margarine and sprinkle with the sesame seeds.

Mixing

- Heat the gelatine mixture in the microwave for 50 seconds.
- Add the yeast and stand for 10 minutes.
- Whisk the eggs, sugar, salt and citric acid in a separate bowl with an electric mixer until stiff.
- Tip the flour into the wet mixture.
- Beat in the oil and whisked eggs for 1 minute with electric mixer.
- Cover the basin and let stand again for 10 minutes.
- Whisk again and pour the mixture into the tin and leave for about 20 minutes to rise

Baking

- Preheat the oven to 200°C (400°F).
- Place in the centre of the oven and bake for 45 minutes.
- Remove from the oven and wrap in a clean tea towel to cool then place in a plastic bag until ready to serve.

Chapatis (India)

Served with a spicy curry these treats will delight your guests. They are also quick and tasty for an after-school snack. Although they are traditionally unleavened the addition of baking powder compensates for the lack of gluten in the flour. They can be made and frozen and reheated under the griller before serving.

Ingredients

100g (4oz) plain yoghurt
1 tbsp olive oil
50mL (1¾fl oz) cold water
230g (8oz) Lola's superfine flour
  (page 7)
1 tsp gluten-free baking powder
1 tsp salt
50g (2oz) feta cheese, finely
  chopped
fine rice flour in a shaker to press
  out the chapati

Preparation

- I use a non-stick fryingpan but the chapatis can be cooked on a griddle.

Mixing

- Combine the yoghurt, oil, water, flour, baking powder and salt and mix to a stiff dough.
- Press out the dough and sprinkle with the feta cheese.
- Knead well, cover and let stand for about 15 minutes.
- Divide into balls and using the fine rice flour sprinkle a board and press out into thin circles to fit your pan.

Cooking

- Prepare the pan with some oil or ghee and heat on a medium heat.
- Place the circle of dough on the hot pan and leave for a short time until it is showing dark patches underneath.
- Turn and cook the other side.
- Place the cooked chapati on a cloth and cover to prevent drying.

Dumplings - Galubski (Russia)

A sweet version can be made by adding sugar instead of the onion and spices. Serve these with fruit or caramel sauce.

Ingredients

300g (10½oz) Lola's superfine flour (page 7)
50g (2oz) rice crumbs
1 tsp gluten-free baking powder
3 eggs
2 tbsp melted margarine
½ tsp caraway or other seeds
½ onion, chopped (optional)

Mixing

- Mix together all ingredients and knead to a smooth dough.
- Allow to stand for 20 minutes.

Cooking

- Shape into small balls and cook in a deep pot of boiling water.
- The dumplings are cooked when they rise to the surface.
- Serve in soup or with stew.

Cornish Splits (England)

These 'splits' are meant to be served in pairs
with strawberry jam and clotted cream.

Ingredients

125mL (4fl oz) warm water
1 tsp psyllium
1 tsp salt
1 tbsp dried yeast
1 egg
450g (16oz) Lola's superfine flour
   (page 7)
30g (1oz) sifted pure icing
   (confectioners') sugar
2 tbsp milk powder
1 tbsp melted margarine

Preparation

- Place the warm water in a large mixing bowl and whisk in the
  psyllium, salt and yeast.
- Set aside to rise for 10 minutes while you prepare the other
  ingredients.
- In a small bowl whisk the egg.
- Weigh the flour and set aside 150g (5oz) of it for rolling the splits.
- Combine the larger portion of flour with the icing sugar and
  milk powder.
- Cover a scone tray with baking paper.

Mixing

- Add the beaten egg and melted margarine to the yeast
  mixture. Set the bowl aside to make egg wash by adding a
  teaspoon of milk.
- Using a knife to avoid over-mixing the splits add the flour
  mixture to the liquids and blend the mixture using a cutting
  action for about 1 minute until the flour is incorporated.
- Cover the bowl and rest for 15 minutes.
- Brush the egg bowl with pastry brush to make the wash and
  set aside to glaze the splits.
- Add half the remaining flour to the risen dough and work in
  with the knife.
- Place the remainder of the flour on a pastry board and tip the
  dough on it.
- Lightly knead to incorporate the flour, adding a little more
  flour if necessary but keep in mind that this is a very soft light
  dough.
- Press the dough out in a thick slab with your fingers and cut
  with a small cutter, turning and tucking in the cut corners to
  avoid re-rolling the dough.
- Place the splits together to support each other on the tray.

Baking

- Preheat the oven to 200°C (400°F).
- Brush the tops of the splits with the egg wash and leave to rise
  for 40 minutes.
- Bake for 15 minutes until golden.

Fruit Muffins (England)

Ingredients

1 cup cold water
3 tbsp sugar
1 tbsp psyllium
1 tbsp gelatine
1 tbsp dried yeast
2 egg whites
1 tsp salt
½ tsp citric acid
250g (8½oz) Lola's superfine flour
  (page 7)
2 tbsp olive oil
1 cup mixed fruit

Preparation

- Place the cold water into a large glass bowl or microwave dish.
- Add the sugar, psyllium and gelatine.
- Let stand for 1 minute to soften.
- Grease the muffin tins with some dairy-free margarine.

Mixing

- Heat the gelatine mixture in the microwave for 50 seconds.
- Add the yeast and stand for 10 minutes.
- Whisk the egg whites, salt and citric acid in a separate bowl with an electric mixer until stiff.
- Tip the dry ingredients into the wet mixture.
- Beat in the oil and whisked eggs for 1 minute with electric mixer.
- Cover and let stand again for 10 minutes.

Baking

- Preheat the oven to 180°C (350°F).
- Spoon a tablespoon of the mixture into the tins, sprinkle with half the fruit, add more batter.
- Then sprinkle with remaining fruit, top with mixture and leave until puffy, about 15 minutes.
- Place in the centre of the oven and bake for 20 minutes.
- Remove from the oven and wrap in a clean tea towel to cool then place in a plastic bag until ready to serve.

Herb Focaccia (Italy)

This mixture can be baked in one or two 20cm (7¾in) round sponge tins depending on the thickness of the bread required. It contains no gluten, wheat, corn or egg (if egg substitute is used).

Ingredients

½ cup cold water
1 tsp gelatine
pinch salt
1 tsp sugar
1 tbsp dried yeast
65mL (2¼fl oz) olive oil
140g (5oz) Lola's superfine flour
   (page 7)
1 egg or egg substitute
1 tsp mixed herbs
1 tsp sesame seeds

Preparation

- Place the cold water in a medium-sized mixing bowl.
- Sprinkle the gelatine on the water and let stand for 2 minutes.
- Grease the sides of the bread pan and cut a circle of baking paper to line the bottom Heat the gelatine in the microwave until clear, about 20 seconds.

Mixing

- Add the salt, sugar and yeast to the warm gelatine, stand 10 minutes.
- Using an electric mixer beat in the oil, flour and egg for about 1 minute to make sure the yeast is well distributed.
- Stir in the mixed herbs.
- Pour the batter into one or two prepared tins and leave the mixture to stand for 20 minutes until bubbles form; it does not rise much in the tin.

Baking

- Preheat the oven to 220°C (420°F).
- Sprinkle the top with sesame seeds and cook for 10–20 minutes depending on thickness.

Kulich – Yeast Cake (Russia)

This bread is traditionally baked in terracotta flowerpots and served with pashka (a sweet cottage-cheese ice cream). I use a 20cm (7¾in) fluted ring tin.

Ingredients

1 tbsp dried yeast
125mL (4fl oz) warm milk
100g (4oz) sugar
½ tsp salt
200g (7oz) Lola's superfine flour
   (page 7)
2 eggs separated
60g (2oz) softened butter
2 tbsp almond meal
1 tsp vanilla essence
3 ground cardamon seeds
1 tsp ground cinnamon
1 tsp ground nutmeg
100g (4oz) raisins
30g (1oz) peel
1 cup hot coffee
2 tbsp vodka

Preparation

- Prepare a tin by greasing with margarine or if using a flowerpot carefully line it with foil.
- Dissolve yeast in warm milk with 1 tablespoon of the sugar, salt and half the flour.
- Mix well, cover and allow to rise until puffy; about 20 minutes.

Mixing

- Beat egg whites and rest of the sugar until stiff and add alternatively with remainder of the flour.
- Add egg yolks and softened butter then beat with electric mixer for 2 minutes.
- Cover and let mixture rise again until doubled, about 20 minutes.
- Punch down and add almond meal, vanilla essence and spices.
- Pour a little mixture into tin, add raisins and peel then more mixture, continuing this method until all the fruit and mixture is used.

Baking

- Preheat the oven to 160°C (320°F).
- Allow cake to stand about 30 minutes or until the tin is three-parts full.
- Cook for 40 minutes.
- Remove from the oven and drizzle the coffee and vodka over the hot cake.
- Cool slightly before serving with ice cream.

Griddle Bread (Ireland)

Cook in a heavy frying pan.

Ingredients

125mL (4fl oz) warm milk
1 tsp sugar
2 tbsp baby rice cereal
200g (7oz) Lola's superfine flour
   (page 7)
2 tsp gluten-free baking powder
2 tbsp olive oil

Mixing

- Place the warm milk in a medium mixing bowl and add the sugar, baby rice cereal, three quarters of the flour and the baking powder. Mix well with a knife.
- Place the remaining flour on a board and tip the bread mix onto it.
- Knead lightly until all the flour is absorbed.
- Oil the basin the bread was mixed in with 1 tablespoon of olive oil.
- Place the dough back in the bowl and roll it around in the oiled basin to cover the surface with oil.
- Cover with a cloth and let rest for 10 minutes.
- Remove from the bowl and flatten on a sheet of plastic to a circle to fit the base of your pan.
- If too sticky use a little fine rice flour to press out the dough.

Cooking

- Oil the pan with the remaining olive oil.
- Preheat your pan to a medium heat and using the plastic sheet to lift the dough, tip it into the pan.
- Adjust the size if necessary by pressing out a little more with your fingers.
- Cut the dough into four quarters with a knife.
- Cook the bread for 3 minutes on the medium heat before turning with a spatula.
- Reduce the pan heat to low and continue to cook for a further 10 minutes until the bread sounds hollow when tapped.

Choux Cheese Bread (France)

Ingredients

320mL (11fl oz) water
1 tsp salt
130g (4½oz) butter
250g (8½oz) Lola's superfine flour
   (page 7)
5 eggs
250g (8½oz) gruyère cheese
30g (1oz) cheddar cheese

Preparation

- Cover a large oven tray with silicone baking paper.

Mixing

- Place the water, salt and butter in a saucepan and bring to boil.
- When boiling add all the flour and combine with a wooden spoon.
- Cook until mixture leaves the side of pan.
- When cool add the eggs one at a time, beating with wooden spoon.
- Chop gruyère into small cubes and grate cheddar.
- Add the gruyère cubes to the pastry and mix well.
- Heap the mixture like a cake, onto the centre of the baking tray.
- Sprinkle with the grated cheddar cheese.

Baking

- Cook for 1 hour at 200°C (400°F).

Panettone (Italy)

Cooked in a traditional tall tin this Italian yeast cake is served with breakfast coffee throughout the year and is used for gift-giving at Christmas. You can make smaller versions by using large fruit cans.

Ingredients

1 tbsp dried yeast
125mL (4fl oz) warm water
100g (4oz) sugar
200g (7oz) Lola's superfine flour
    (page 7)
2 eggs separated
½ tsp salt
60g (2oz) softened butter
2 tsp vanilla essence
100g (4oz) sultanas
50g (2oz) mixed peel

Preparation

- Prepare a deep tin by greasing with margarine.
- Dissolve yeast in warm water with 1 tablespoon of the sugar and half the flour.
- Mix well, cover and allow to rise until puffy; about 20 minutes.

Mixing

- Beat egg whites, salt and remaining sugar until stiff and add alternatively with remainder of the flour.
- Add egg yolks and softened butter then beat with electric mixer for 2 minutes.
- Cover and let mixture rise again until doubled, about 20 minutes.
- Punch down and add the vanilla essence.
- Pour a little mixture into tin, add sultanas and peel then more mixture, continuing this method until all the fruit and mixture is used.

Baking

- Preheat the oven to 160°C (320°F).
- Allow mixture to stand for about 30 minutes or until the tin is three-parts full.
- Cook for 40 minutes on low shelf.

Pumpernickel (Denmark)

This recipe is steamed in a small bread tin 18 x 11 x 10cm deep (7 x 4 x 4in) inside a larger tin that is filled with water.

Ingredients

375mL (13fl oz) boiling water
60g (2oz) fine polenta (corn meal)
1 tsp salt
¼ cup molasses
65mL (2¼fl oz) olive oil
100g (4oz) Lola's superfine flour (page 7)
50g (2oz) brown rice flour
1 tbsp dried yeast
1 egg
1 tbsp carob
1 tsp parisian essence
1 tbsp caraway seeds

Preparation

- Place the boiling water in a saucepan and slowly whisk the polenta into the rapidly boiling water.
- Cook for a few minutes until smooth.
- Add the salt, molasses and oil and leave to cool slightly.
- Grease a small bread tin with some margarine and line it with silicone baking paper.

Mixing

- Add half the flour, brown rice flour and the yeast to the warm mixture and stand for 15 minutes.
- Whisk in the egg, remaining flour, carob and Parisian essence with an electric mixer.
- Stir in caraway seeds.
- Cover and let stand again for 15 minutes.

Baking

- Preheat the oven to 150°C (300°F).
- Place the large tin half-full of hot water in the oven.
- Pour the bread mixture into the small tin and leave for about 30 minutes to rise.
- Place the small tin in the water bath and cook for 2 hours.
- Remove from the oven and cool in the tin.
- Wrap in a clean tea towel and refrigerate overnight before cutting.

Sourdough Loaf (America)

I use a high loaf tin to bake this loaf. Because it has only been allowed to rise once it has a coarse texture. Knocking back after 15 minutes of the first rise and allowing it to rise for 30 minutes again before baking can refine the texture.

Ingredients

125mL (4fl oz) sourdough starter (see below)
125mL (4fl oz) warm water
200g (7oz) Lola's superfine flour (page 7)
1 tsp salt
1 tsp sugar
1 tsp dried yeast
1 egg

Preparation

- Select and grease your bread tin.
- Preheat the oven to 180°C (350°F).

Mixing

- Place the starter in a medium-sized bowl and add all the other ingredients.
- Beat with an electric mixer for 2 minutes.
- Pour into the greased tin and allow to rise for 30 minutes.

Baking

- Place on a low shelf in the oven and bake for 40 minutes.
- Cool and refrigerate before slicing.

Starter for sourdough

2 tbsp dried yeast
1 cup lukewarm water
180g (6oz) Lola's superfine flour (page 7)
1 tsp sugar
1 tsp salt

Preparation

- Place in a jar and leave for at least 48 hours.
- Stir twice daily.
- Use up to a third of mixture to make sourdough bread.
- Replace used starter with equal quantities of flour and water and do not use again for another 48 hours.

Yellow Corn Bread (America)

This loaf is free of yeast.

Ingredients

150mL (5fl oz) warm water
2 tbsp softened margarine
2 eggs
100g (4oz) Lola's superfine flour
  (page 7)
100g (4oz) yellow maize flour
2 tbsp milk powder
1 tbsp psyllium
1 tsp salt
1 tbsp gluten-free baking powder
1 tbsp poppy seeds

Preparation

- Preheat the oven to 200°C (400°F).
- Grease the oven tray or cover with baking paper.

Mixing

- Place the warm water in a medium-sized mixing bowl and add the softened margarine.
- Lightly beat the eggs and add to bowl.
- Add all the remaining ingredients and mix well to a soft batter.
- Beat for at least 1 minute with a wooden spoon or mixer.

Baking

- Pour onto the baking tray and finish with poppy seeds.
- Cook on a middle shelf for about 15 minutes.
- Remove from the oven and cool on a wire rack covered with a damp tea towel.

Spring Roll Wraps (China)

These wraps can be made in advance and frozen in
aluminium foil.
Defrost at room temperature before use.

Ingredients

1 cup warm water
2 tsp salt
2 tsp psyllium
200g (7oz) Lola's superfine flour
   (page 7)
3 tbsp olive oil

Suggested fillings

lightly cooked minced beef,
chicken or pork mince
shredded chinese cabbage
sprouts
sliced onion
any chinese vegetables
season as desired with sauce or salt
and pepper

Preparation

- I used a non-stick omelette pan but if you don't have one you can season a steel frying pan by burning a nob of butter in it, wiping clean and regreasing with a buttered paper towel.
- A low to medium heat is required to cook the wraps as they should not colour.

Mixing

- Place the warm water, salt and psyllium in a bowl, using a wire whisk add the flour and oil.
- Leave to stand for 5 minutes while you prepare the pan.

Making

- If using a non-stick pan wipe it out with a paper towel and a small amount of oil to remove any particles that can cause the wraps to stick. Heat the pan to a medium heat.
- Pour about ¼ cup (depending on the size of the pan) of mixture in the centre of the pan, lift the pan and roll the mixture around to cover the base with a thin layer.
- Leave to set for about 1 minute; until it will slide in the pan.
- Tip out on a cloth to cool and cover to prevent drying.
- When cool, store in a plastic bag in the refrigerator until you are ready to fill them.

Cooking the spring rolls

- Lay the wraps flat and spoon filling onto the centre.
- Brush the edges with a little egg white.
- Turn in the ends, parcel style, and roll up to seal.
- Deep-fry in olive oil for a few minutes until golden.

Note: The filled spring rolls can be frozen and cooked straight from the freezer as required.

Barbari Pockets

This Persian bread is ideal filled with salad for lunches. Fine rice flour in a sprinkler canister is useful for all gluten free pastry rolling.

Ingredients

200mL (7fl oz) warm water
1 tsp honey
1 tsp gelatine
2 tsp psyllium
1 tsp salt
1 tbsp dried yeast
300g (10½oz) Lola's superfine flour (page 7)
1 tsp paprika
½ tsp cayenne pepper
3 tbsp olive oil
extra ¼ cup fine rice flour for rolling

Preparation

- Place the warm water in a bowl and add the honey, gelatine, psyllium, salt and yeast.
- Stir with a fork, cover and leave to stand for 5 minutes.
- Cut four saucer-size, about 15cm diameter, circles of baking paper.
- Also cut one piece of plastic the same size to use to shape the tops.
- Preheat a heavy flat oven tray in a 180°C (350°F) oven.

Mixing

- Add half the flour to the yeast mixture.
- Cover and stand to rise for 10 minutes.
- Add the remainder of the flour, spices and oil.
- Mix well with a knife using a cutting action and tip onto a board.
- Knead for a few minutes until smooth, using the rice flour if necessary.

Making the pockets

- Divide the dough into four balls.
- Press out half a ball on each paper, using your fingers with a little rice flour if necessary.
- Cover with a cloth to prevent drying. Place them on the baking tray.
- Smear the plastic circle with some extra oil.
- Place half a ball of dough on the oiled sheet and press out to fit the prepared pocket bottom on the paper. Brush halfway around the bottom circle with water to stick the top and leave an opening. Top the bottom dough portions with the 'lid' and peel back the oiled plastic to use again to make the next lid. Continue with this method to make three more tops.

Baking

- Cover the prepared pockets with a cloth and leave to stand about for 20 minutes.
- Brush with a little oil. Cook for 5 minutes in the preheated oven, then reduce the heat and cook for another 3 minutes. Remove from the oven and wrap in a cloth and place in a plastic bag to cool. Note: Baking paper circles can be reused next time.

Bubble Bread Squares

These make good lunch biscuits for savoury spreads such as peanut butter.

Ingredients

30g (1oz) butter
65mL (2¼fl oz) warm water
1 tsp dried yeast
1 tsp salt
1 tsp sugar
140g (5oz) Lola's superfine flour
  (page 7)
2 tbsp arrowroot

Preparation

- Cut a sheet of baking paper to fit your baking tray.
- Chop butter into small pieces.
- Preheat the oven to 200°C (400°F).

Mixing

- Place the warm water into a mixing bowl.
- Add the yeast, salt and sugar.
- Stand for 10 minutes.
- Stir in the flour and arrowroot and add the chopped butter.
- Blend together to make a stiff dough.

Cutting the squares

- Roll out on the baking paper using a small sheet of lightly oiled plastic to cover the dough.
- Don't use cling wrap, an opened plastic bag is better if you don't have a pastry sheet.
- Roll the pastry as thin as possible in an oblong shape.
- Remove the plastic sheet and prick well with a skewer to prevent uneven rising.
- Cut into squares using a square cutter or a knife.
- Remove excess dough to re-roll.

Baking

- Lift the baking paper holding the squares onto your oven tray.
- Stand for 10 minutes.
- Brush with cold water and sprinkle with salt.
- Bake for 10–15 minutes.
- Cool and store in an airtight jar.

Tip: The base of a springform tin makes a good tool for lifting the squares on to the baking tray.

Corn Flatbread

Use a lamington or slice tray 25 x 18 x 3cm deep (10 x 7 x 1in). For lovers of traditional cornbread this heavy bread is best served warm. The crisp flatbread will keep fresh in a jar for two or three days. The mixture appears to be very thin but this is correct to give you a wafer-thin, crisp flatbread rather like potato crisps.

Ingredients

1 tsp salt
1 tsp sugar
1 tbsp dried yeast
1 cup warm water
65mL (2¼fl oz) olive oil
1 tbsp psyllium
200g (7oz) yellow maize flour
50g (2oz) arrowroot
1 egg

Preparation

- Place the salt, sugar and yeast into the warm water, and stand for 10 minutes to rise.
- Preheat the oven to 200°C (400°F). Grease the tin with margarine.

Mixing

- Add the olive oil, psyllium, maize flour, arrowroot and egg.
- Beat the mixture with an electric beater for about 1 minute. The mixture should be a thick batter.

Baking

- Pour the mixture into the prepared tin, and leave to rise for 30 minutes.
- Bake for 20 minutes. Cool before cutting.

Tip: Thinning the batter with more warm water will give a lighter bread.

Pita Bread

I cooked these pita breads on ceramic glazed tiles on the oven wire racks.
These can be bought at any tile shop, unglazed are best.

Ingredients

125mL (4fl oz) cold water
1 tsp gelatine
2 tsp psyllium
1 tbsp dried yeas
1 tsp salt
1 tsp sugar
2 tbsp olive oil
200g (7oz) Lola's superfine flour
  (page 7)

Preparation

- Place the cold water in a medium-sized glass or china bowl.
- Sprinkle the gelatine and psyllium on top of the water and let stand for 1 minute to soften.
- Cut four oval-shaped pieces of baking paper about 22cm (8½in).
- Place two large ceramic tiles in your oven on the wire racks.
- Heat the oven and tiles to 220°C (420°F).

Mixing

- Heat the gelatine psylllium mix 30 seconds in microwave oven.
- Add the yeast, sugar and salt to the warm water.
- Leave to stand 10 minutes until puffy.
- Add half the flour and mix well with a knife.
- Tip the oil in on the dough and work as though kneading using a heavy plastic spatula or wooden spoon.
- Continue this kneading process for about 5 minutes until the oil is absorbed.
- Cover and leave to stand 10 minutes.
- Turn onto a lightly floured plastic sheet and knead for 5 minutes using the remainder of the flour. Use the plastic to knead by lifting and folding the dough through the plastic.

Shaping

- Divide dough into four teardrop shapes.
- Press out on the oval paper using a plastic sheet and a few drops of oil.
- Cover the ovals with a cloth to rise for 20 minutes.

Baking

- An oven glove is helpful to prevent your hands burning.
- If possible slide out the wire holding the tile.
- Using a metal spatula or egg slice to lift the pitas, place pitas on hot tiles, brush with oil and return to oven.
- Cook for 3 minutes lower heat to 200°C (400°F) and leave for another 1 minute until puffed and slightly golden.
- These breads are meant to be chewy and moist; cool in a plastic bag to prevent drying.

Feta Florentine Slab

Ingredients

1 cup warm water
1 tsp salt
1 tsp sugar
1 tbsp dried yeast
100g (4oz) feta cheese
250g (8½oz) Lola's superfine flour
   (page 7)
1 egg white
1 cup chopped spinach
extra cheese or seeds for topping

Preparation

- Preheat the oven to 200°C (400°F).
- Place the warm water in a bowl and add the salt, sugar and yeast.
- Let stand for 10 minutes.
- Grease a 18 x 26 x 3cm (7 x 10 x 1in) deep slab tin with margarine or line it with baking paper.
- Chop or crumble the feta cheese.

Mixing

- Add the flour, and beat for 1 minute with an electric mixer.
- Cover and leave to rise until puffy; about 10 minutes.
- Beat the egg white, add to mixture and whisk again for 1 minute.
- Pour half the mixture into prepared tin.
- Arrange the chopped spinach leaves on the batter.
- Top with the crumbled feta cheese, and cover with remaining bread mixture.
- Let stand to rise for another 10 minutes.
- Sprinkle with seeds or grated cheese.

Baking

- Bake for 25 minutes.

Olive Hearth Bread

This Italian treat is usually made as a family loaf for eating while fresh. This loaf can be made in any shallow tin; it is a spectacular addition to any meal.

Ingredients

1 cup warm water
1 tsp salt
 tsp sugar
1 tbsp dried yeast
250g (8½oz) Lola's superfine flour (page 7)
1 egg
1 cup seeded olives
1 tsp fresh rosemary
1 cup grated gruyère cheese
sesame seeds for garnish

Preparation

- Preheat the oven to 200°C (400°F).
- Place the warm water in a bowl and add the salt, sugar and yeast.
- Let stand for 10 minutes.
- Grease a bread tin with margarine and line it with sesame seeds.

Mixing

- Add the flour, and beat for 1 minute with an electric mixer.
- Cover and leave to rise until puffy; about 10 minutes.
- Beat the egg white, add to mixture and beat again for 1 minute.
- Pour into prepared tin and let stand to rise for another 10 minutes.
- Top with the olives and rosemary.
- Cover with grated cheese.

Baking

- Bake for 15–20 minutes.

Naan Flats

This method will allow you to produce a reasonable gluten-free version of naan bread. Grilled on ovals of baking paper on a preheated oven tray it is served hot with traditional Indian dishes such as tandoori chicken.

Ingredients

125mL (4fl oz) milk
1 tsp sugar
1 tsp salt
1 tsp gelatine
1 tbsp dried yeast
250g (8½oz) Lola's superfine flour (page 7)
1 tsp bicarbonate of soda
2 tbsp olive oil

Preparation

- Place the milk in a glass or china bowl.
- Add the sugar, salt and sprinkle on the gelatine.
- Leave to stand for 1 minute.
- Heat in microwave for 30 seconds.
- Remove from microwave and add the yeast to the warm milk. Stand for 10 minutes.
- Cut four tear-shaped ovals about 21 x 16cm (8¼ x 6¼in) of heavy baking paper or foil.
- Preheat a flat oven tray under a hot griller.

Mixing

- Add the flour, bicarbonate of soda and oil to the yeast mixture and mix well to form a light dough.
- Tip out on a board and knead lightly using a little more flour if necessary. Be careful not to add too much extra flour, as this will dry your breads.

Baking

- Heat the griller to its highest temperature.
- Divide dough into four pieces and press out on the shaped papers.
- Cover with a cloth and leave to stand for 10 minutes.
- Brush the breads with cold water and place under the hot griller for 3–4 minutes until bubbled and brown.
- Remove from oven and stack covered by a cloth to prevent drying.

Potato Griddle Bread

Cooked in a heavy frying pan this bread makes a quick alternative base for a snack such as sautéed mushrooms and bacon. One medium-sized potato produces approximately 60g (2oz) mashed potato.

Ingredients

125mL (4fl oz) warm water
1 tsp sugar
1 tsp salt
2 tsp dried yeast
40g warm mashed potato
200g (7oz) Lola's superfine flour
   (page 7)
2 tbsp olive oil

Preparation

- Place the warm water in a medium mixing bowl and add the sugar, salt and yeast.
- Stir in the mashed potato and leave to rise for 10 minutes.

Mixing

- Add three quarters of the flour to the yeast and mix well.
- Place the remaining flour on a board and tip the bread mix onto it.
- Knead lightly until all the flour is absorbed.
- Oil the bowl the bread was mixed in with 1 tablespoon of olive oil.
- Place the dough back in the bowl and roll it around in the oiled basin to cover the surface with oil.
- Cover with a cloth and let rest for 20 minutes.
- Remove from the bowl and flatten on a sheet of plastic to a circle to fit the base of your frying pan.
- If too sticky use a little fine rice flour to press out the dough.

Cooking

- Oil the pan with the remaining olive oil.
- Preheat your pan to a medium heat and using the plastic sheet to lift the dough, tip it into the pan. Adjust the size if necessary by pressing out a little more with your fingers.
- Cut the dough into four quarters with a knife.
- Cook the bread for 3 minutes on medium heat before turning with a spatula.
- Reduce the pan heat to low and continue to cook for a further 10 minutes until the bread sounds hollow when tapped.

Pumpkin Wraps

These pumpkin wraps are cooked in the oven on a circle
of baking paper on a 30cm (11¾in) pizza tray. The mixture
should be thin enough to pour and easily cover the pizza tray,
if not add a little more warm water.

Ingredients

2 cups warm water
1 tbsp dried yeast
1 tsp sugar
1 tsp salt
250g (8½oz) Lola's superfine flour
   (page 7)
1 tbsp gelatine
125mL (4fl oz) olive oil
1 egg
½ cup cooked mashed pumpkin

Preparation

- Place the warm water in a mixing bowl.
- Add the yeast, sugar and salt and let rise for 10 minutes.
- Cut four circles of baking paper to fit the pizza tray.
- Preheat the oven to 200°C (400°F).

Mixing

- Stir in the flour, gelatine and oil to the yeast mixture.
- Whisk in the egg with a rotary or wire whisk.
- Cover and let rise for 15 minutes.
- Add the mashed pumpkin and whisk until the mixture is flat,
  about 30 seconds.

Baking

- Pour about a cup of the mixture onto the baking paper circles
  on the tray.
- Spread well to form a thin circle.
- Cook for about 2 minutes until set.
- Remove from oven and cover with foil or a plastic bag.
- Note: These wraps will keep well in a plastic bag in the
  refrigerator for several days. Warm for a few seconds in the
  microwave before filling.

Quick Focaccia

Use a lamington or slice tray 25 x 18 x 3cm (deep. As there is no oil or gelatine in this loaf it will not keep long but it is great to eat while warm to accompany salads or a barbecue. It is also good for bruschetta.

Ingredients

1 cup warm water
1 tsp salt
1 tsp sugar
1 tbsp dried yeast
250g (8½oz) Lola's superfine flour (page 7)
1 egg white
sesame seeds or grated cheese for garnish

Preparation

- Place the warm water in a bowl and add the salt, sugar and yeast.
- Let stand for 10 minutes.
- Grease a small bread tin with margarine and line it with seeds or baking paper.

Mixing

- Add the flour, and beat for 1 minute with an electric mixer.
- Cover and leave to rise until puffy about 10 minutes.
- Beat the egg white, add to the mixture and beat again for 1 minute.
- Pour into prepared tin and let stand to rise for another 10 minutes.
- Sprinkle with seeds or grated cheese if preferred.

Baking

- Bake at 200°C (400°F) for 25 minutes.

Red Onion Flatbread

Use a lamington or slice tray 25 x 18 x 3cm (10 x 7 x 1in) deep. This flatbread is meant to be eaten warm and is a quick treat to serve with a seafood salad lunch. If you wish to use this when entertaining make yourself a premix of the all dry ingredients that can be added to the warm water an hour before the guests arrive.

Ingredients

125mL (4fl oz) cold water
125mL (4fl oz) boiling water
1 tbsp dried yeast
1 tbsp gelatine
1 tsp salt
1 tbsp sugar
1 tbsp psyllium
½ tsp citric acid
300g Lola's superfine flour (page 7)
2 egg whites
1 large red onion, sliced
50g (2oz) grated mozzarella cheese
paprika for sprinkling

Preparation

- Grease a slice tray well with margarine. Line with baking paper.
- Place the water, hot and cold, into a medium-sized glass or plastic bowl.
- Lightly whisk in yeast, gelatine, salt, sugar and psyllium.
- Cover the bowl and leave to rise for 15 minutes.

Mixing

- Add the citric acid and flour to the liquids and beat with an electric mixer for about 1 minute.
- Cover the bowl with a large plastic bag; no need to remove the beater. Leave to rise for 20 minutes.
- Add the egg whites and beat the mixture for 1 minute, then pour into the prepared tin.
- Arrange large rings of red onion on top and cover with the grated mozzarella cheese.
- Sprinkle with paprika.
- Preheat the oven to 200°C (400°F).
- Cover the tin with the plastic bag and leave to rise for 25 minutes.

Baking

- Bake on the lower shelf for 30 minutes.
- Remove from oven and wrap in a clean tea towel.
- Serve warm.

Sourdough Flatbread

This is a sourdough flatbread baked in a large shallow round tin. The soft chewy centre and crunchy crust is well worth the effort of making the sourdough starter.

Ingredients

½ cup sourdough starter (see below)
125mL (4fl oz) warm water
200g (7oz) Lola's superfine flour (page 7)
1 tsp salt
1 tsp sugar
1 tsp dried yeast
1 egg

Preparation

- Select and grease your bread tin.
- Preheat the oven to 200°C (400°F).

Mixing

- Place the starter in a medium-sized bowl and add all the other ingredients.
- Beat with an electric mixer for 2 minutes.
- Allow to rise for 30 minutes in the bowl; no need to remove the beaters.
- Knock back by beating for 1 minute.
- Pour into the greased tin and allow to rise for 30 minutes.
- Top with your favourite smoked or flavoured cheese.

Baking

- Place on a high shelf in the oven and bake for 30 minutes.
- Enjoy with salad while warm.

Starter for sourdough

2 tbsp dried yeast
1 cup lukewarm water
180g (6oz) Lola's superfine flour (page 7)
1 tsp sugar
1 tsp salt

Preparation

- Place in a jar and leave for at least 48 hours. Stir twice daily.
- Use up one-third of mixture to make sourdough bread.
- Replace used starter with equal quantities of flour and water and do not use again for another 24 hours.

Sundried Tomato Bread

Use a lamington or slice tray 25 x 18 x 3cm (10 x 7 x 1in) deep. As there is no oil or gelatine in this loaf it will not keep long but it is great to eat while warm to accompany salads or a barbecue.

Ingredients

1 cup warm water
1 tsp salt
1 tsp sugar
1 tbsp dried yeast
½ cup soft sundried tomatoes
250g (8½oz) Lola's superfine flour
   (page 7)
1 egg white
sesame seeds or grated cheese for
   garnish

Preparation

- Preheat the oven to 200°C (400°F).
- Place the warm water in a bowl and add the salt, sugar and yeast.
- Let stand for 10 minutes.
- Drain the sundried tomatoes on kitchen paper to remove excess oil.
- Grease a slice tin with margarine and line it with seeds or baking paper.

Mixing

- Add the flour, and beat for 1 minute with an electric mixer.
- Cover and leave to rise until puffy about 10 minutes.
- Beat the egg white, add to the mixture and beat again for 1 minute.
- Pour half the mixture into prepared tin and arrange the tomatoes on top.
- Cover with remaining bread mixture and let stand to rise for another 10 minutes.
- Sprinkle with seeds or grated cheese if preferred.

Baking

- Bake for 25 minutes.

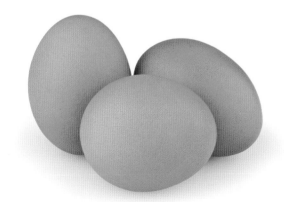

White Wraps

These yeasted wraps are great for lunches and will keep fresh in a plastic bag for two or three days. The mixture appears to be very thin but this is correct to cover the base of the pan or pizza tray and give you a thin wrap; a thicker mixture will look more like a pancake.

Ingredients

2 cups warm water
1 tbsp dried yeast
1 tsp sugar
1 tsp salt
250g (8½oz) Lola's superfine flour (page 7)
1 tbsp gelatine
125mL (4fl oz) olive oil
1 egg

Preparation

- Place the warm water in a mixing bowl.
- Add the yeast, sugar and salt and let rise for 10 minutes.
- Grease a large frying pan or the base of a camp oven with margarine.

Mixing

- Stir in the flour, gelatine and oil.
- Whisk in the egg with a rotary or wire whisk.
- Cover and let rise for 15 minutes.
- Whisk until the mixture is flat, about 30 seconds.

Baking

- Heat the pan to a medium heat.
- Pour about a cup of the mixture into the greased pan.
- Spread well to form a large circle.
- Cook for a few minutes until set.
- Loosen with a spatula and turn.
- Flatten by pressing down with the base of a large saucepan.
- Cook for about 2 minutes.
- Remove from pan and cover with foil or a plastic bag.

Oven baking

- Pour ¾ cup of batter on to a greased 30cm (11¾in) round pizza tray and bake for 6 minutes at 180°C (350°F) until firm.
- Cool for a minute on the tray and tip onto a tea towel; cover well to prevent drying.
- Store in a large plastic bag in the refrigerator.

Crisp Flatbread

Ingredients

1 cup warm water
2 tsp psyllium
50g (2oz) Lola's superfine flour
 (page 7)
50g (2oz) tapioca starch
1 tsp salt

Preparation

- Preheat the oven to 230°C (445°F). Place the warm water in a mixing bowl.
- Sprinkle the psyllium onto the water and mix and let stand for 1 minute.
- Cut a piece of baking paper 30 x 20cm (11¾ x 7¾in) and place on a flat baking tray.

Mixing

- Stir the dry ingredients in to the warm water and leave to rise for 10 minutes.
- Whisk the mixture using a wire whisk.

Baking

- Pour half the batter onto the paper and let stand for 10 minutes.
- Place in the oven and bake for 10–15 minutes until golden and crisp.
- Remove from the paper and cook the second bread on the same paper.

Yeast-free Focaccia

This recipe does not contain yeast, wheat, gluten or dairy. I use a 20cm (7¾in) sandwich pan. One medium-sized potato produces approximately 60g (2oz) mashed potato.

Ingredients

65mL (2¼fl oz) hot water
65mL (2¼fl oz) olive oil
1 egg or substitute
150g (5oz) Lola's superfine flour
 (page 7)
1 tsp salt
1 tsp gluten-free baking powder
100g (4oz) soft mashed potato
1 tsp sesame seeds

Preparation

- Grease the sides of the pan and cut a circle of baking paper to line the bottom.
- Preheat the oven to 200°C (400°F).

Mixing

- Place the hot water, oil and lightly whisked egg into a bowl and sift in the flour, salt and baking powder.
- Beat the mixture with a rotary whisk for about 1 minute, then add the mashed potato.
- Pour the batter into the prepared cake pan. Sprinkle with sesame seeds.

Baking

- Let stand for 10 minutes.
- Cook for 10–15 minutes.

Kids' Collection

Apple and Walnut Sticks

You will need an éclair tray to cook these sticks.

Ingredients

200mL (7fl oz) cold water
1 tsp salt
1 tsp sugar
1 tbsp gelatine
1 tbsp dried yeast
280g Lola's superfine flour (page 7)
2 tbsp baby rice cereal
1 egg
1 tbsp olive oil
1 apple, coarsely grated
100g (4oz) walnuts

Preparation

- Place the cold water into a large glass bowl or microwave dish.
- Add the salt, sugar and gelatine.
- Let stand for 1 minute to soften.
- Grease the éclair tray with some margarine.
- Heat the gelatine mixture in the microwave for 40 seconds.
- Preheat the oven to 180°C (350°F).

Mixing

- Stir the yeast in to the warm gelatine mixture and let stand for 3 minutes.
- Add flour, rice cereal, egg and olive oil.
- Beat the mixture for 1 minute with an electric mixer.
- Let stand for 5 minutes.
- Whisk again and spoon 1 tablespoon of mixture into each pan spreading up the side a little to prevent the filling sticking to the tin.
- Top the mixture with a tablespoon of grated apple and some walnuts.
- Cover with another tablespoon of mixture.
- Leave to rise for 10 minutes before baking.

Baking

- Bake for 10 minutes.

Currant Dumplings

Ingredients

½ cup cold water
1 tsp gelatine
40g chopped suet or butter
½ cup currants
1 tsp salt
1 tsp gluten-free baking powder
60g (2oz) Lola's superfine flour
   (page 7)
30g (1oz) fine rice crumbs

Preparation

- Place the cold water into a bowl; add the gelatine, suet and currants.
- Combine all the ingredients, using a knife to avoid overmixing.
- Roll into balls, using a little more flour if the mixture is too moist.
- Place the balls into the simmering water, cover with a lid and gently cook for at least 40 minutes, or up to an hour.
- It is important to keep the dumplings boiling to prevent them becoming soggy.
- Serve warm with caramel syrup (see below).

Caramel syrup

60g (2oz) butter
60g (2oz) brown sugar
1 tbsp golden syrup
65mL (2¼fl oz) cold water or milk

Preparation

- Melt the butter and brown sugar over a low heat until it is golden.
- Add the golden syrup and boil rapidly for a few seconds.
- Thin with the cold water or milk.

Baby Rusks

You will need a sponge finger tray to cook these rusks. Dried egg white or egg replacer may be used in place of bread improver. Fresh egg white will make the rusks too soft.

Ingredients

125mL (4fl oz) warm water
1 tsp sugar
1 tsp salt
2 tsp dried yeast
160g (5½oz) Lola's superfine flour (page 7)
2 tsp Lola's bread improver
1 tsp gelatine
2 tbsp olive oil

Preparation

- Place the warm water into a medium-sized mixing bowl.
- Add the sugar, salt and dried yeast, and stir with a fork.
- Leave to stand until the mixture froths, about 5 minutes.
- Grease the sponge finger trays.

Mixing

- Add the remaining dry ingredients to the frothy yeast mixture and whisk well.
- Cover the bowl and set aside to stand for 15 minutes.
- Add the olive oil and whisk again.

Baking

- Spoon or pipe the mixture into the sponge finger trays.
- Stand for 10 minutes.
- Preheat the oven to 160°C (320°F).
- Cook for 20 minutes.
- Cool and store in an airtight container.

Dairy-free Bread Pudding

This pudding is egg-free if egg replacer is used. The use of sauce block here will replace the milk and prevent the pudding from curdling.

Ingredients

1 cup boiling water
2 tbsp sugar
pinch salt
1 sauce block (see below)
2 eggs
1 slice gluten-free bread
1 tbsp dairy-free margarine
1 tbsp sultanas
nutmeg for sprinkling
1 vanilla bean or 1 tsp vanilla
    essence

Preparation

- Place the water, sugar and salt into a bowl.
- Add the sauce block and leave to melt.
- Preheat the oven to 150°C (300°F).

Mixing

- Whisk the sauce.
- Beat the eggs and add to (or 1 tablespoon egg replacer with 2 tablespoons water) to sauce.
- Add the vanilla as desired.
- Spread the bread with the margarine, remove crusts and cut in eight pieces.
- Place the sultanas in a small ovenproof dish and arrange the bread over it.
- Pour the sauce over the bread and sprinkle with nutmeg.

Baking

- Place on a low shelf and cook for 20 minutes or until set.

Sauce blocks

140mL (5fl oz) Lola's superfine flour (page 7)
140mL (5fl oz) dairy-free margarine

Preparation

- Cook together for a few minutes and pour into an iceblock tray.
- Freeze or refrigerate until required.
- One block thickens half a cup of liquid for a thin basic sauce.

Finger Bread

Ideal for parties or a gift to a coeliac child. The ends of these sticks are dipped in white chocolate and finished with coloured sprinkles.

Ingredients

65mL (2¼fl oz) water
1 tsp gelatine
1 tsp sugar
1 tsp salt
1 tbsp dried yeast
80g Lola's superfine flour (page 7)
1 tbsp olive oil
coloured sprinkles
white chocolate for dipping

Preparation

- Place the water, gelatine, sugar and salt into a medium-sized mixing bowl.
- Heat in microwave for 30 seconds.
- Stir in the yeast.
- Leave to stand until the mixture froths, about 5 minutes.
- Cover a baking tray with silicone baking paper.

Mixing

- Add the half remaining dry ingredients and olive oil to the frothy yeast mixture and mix well.
- Tip the remaining flour onto a board and knead it into the dough.
- Shape into 12 sticks and place on the baking tray to rise for 30 minutes.
- Preheat oven to 180°C (350°F).

Baking

- Cook for 10–15 minutes.
- Cool and store in an airtight container.
- Finish with the tips dipped in melted white chocolate and sprinkles if desired.
- Tip for chocolate melting: Melt chocolate in a bowl over hot water.
- Keep covered with a lid to prevent any steam entering the bowl as this will spoil the chocolate.

Lunch Buns

You will need a set of six large muffin pans to cook these buns. One medium-sized potato produces approximately 60g (2oz) mashed potato.

Ingredients

200mL (7fl oz) cold water
1 tsp of salt
1 tsp of sugar
1 tbsp gelatine
60g (2oz) soft mashed potato
1 tbsp dried yeast
280g (10oz) Lola's superfine flour
   (page 7)
1 egg
1 tbsp olive oil
poppy seeds for topping

Filling

½ cup corn kernels
1 small onion, sliced
½ green capsicum, chopped
2 tbsp chopped ham or bacon

Preparation

- Place the cold water into a large glass bowl or microwave dish.
- Add the salt, sugar and gelatine.
- Let stand for 1 minute to soften.
- Grease six individual large muffin tins with some dairy-free margarine.
- Heat the gelatine mixture in the microwave for 50 seconds.
- Preheat the oven to 200°C (400°F).

Mixing

- Whisk the mashed potato into the hot gelatine mixture.
- Stir in the yeast and let stand for 3 minutes.
- Add flour, egg and olive oil.
- Beat the mixture for 1 minute with an electric mixer.
- Let the mixture stand for 5 minutes.
- Whisk again and spoon 1 tablespoon of mixture into each tin spreading up the side a little to prevent the filling sticking to the tin.
- Top the bread mixture with a tablespoon of corn and a small amount of onion, capsicum and ham.
- Cover with another tablespoon of bread batter.
- Leave to rise for 10 minutes before baking.
- Sprinkle with poppy seeds.

Baking

- Bake for 15 minutes

Mini Pizzas

I cook these mini pizzas on ceramic glazed tiles on the oven wire racks. The tiles can be bought at any tile shop; unglazed are best. If you prefer to use an oven tray, increase the baking time to 10 minutes.

Pizzas

125mL (4fl oz) cold water
1 tsp gelatine
2 tsp psyllium
1 tbsp dried yeast
1 tsp sugar
1 tsp salt
300g (10½oz) Lola's superfine flour
  (page 7)
3 tbsp olive oil

Topping

1 can chopped peeled tomatoes
mixed herbs, fresh if possible
½ cup grated mozzarella cheese
½ cup grated tasty cheese
slices of gluten-free salami or bacon
chopped capsicum (bell pepper)
sliced onion
sliced mushrooms

Preparation

- Place the cold water in a medium-sized glass or china bowl.
- Sprinkle the gelatine and psyllium on top of the water and let stand for 1 minute to soften.
- Cut 12 x 11cm (4¾ x 4¾in) circles of baking paper.
- Place two large ceramic tiles in your oven on the wire racks.
- Heat the oven and tiles to 200°C (400°F).

Mixing

- Heat the gelatine mixture for 30 seconds in microwave oven.
- Add the yeast, sugar and salt to the warm water.
- Leave to stand for 10 minutes until puffy. Add half the flour and mix well with a knife.
- Tip the oil in on the dough and work as though kneading with a heavy plastic spatula.
- Continue this kneading process for about 5 minutes. Cover. Leave to stand for 10 minutes.
- Turn onto a lightly floured board and knead for 5 minutes using the remainder of the flour.
- A sheet of plastic is helpful to knead the dough.

Shaping

- Divide dough into 12 balls.
- Press out on the paper using your fingers dipped in flour or oil.
- Cover the circles with a cloth while you prepare the topping.

Baking

- Boil the tomatoes and herbs together for a few minutes to reduce the juice.
- Spread over the dough rounds.
- Arrange the topping roughly on the pizzas starting and finishing with cheese.
- Cook for 5 minutes, lower heat and leave for another 1 minute until puffed.

Pumpkin Mini Loaves

These loaves look wonderful cooked in tiny loaf tins.
Pumpkin seeds from the pumpkin will cook well on top of the
loaf.

Ingredients

200mL (7fl oz) cold water
1 tsp salt
1 tsp sugar
1 tbsp gelatine
60g (2oz) mashed pumpkin
1 tbsp dried yeast
250g (8½oz) Lola's superfine flour
    (page 7)
1 tsp turmeric
30g (1oz) brown rice flour
1 egg or equivalent egg replacer
2 tbsp olive oil
pumpkin seeds for top

Preparation

- Place the cold water into a large glass bowl or microwave dish.
- Add the salt, sugar and gelatine.
- Let stand for 1 minute to soften.
- Grease four mini bread pans with some dairy-free margarine.
- Heat the gelatine mixture in the microwave for 50 seconds.

Mixing

- Add the mashed pumpkin to the hot gelatine mixture.
- Stir in the yeast and whisk slightly. Let stand for 5 minutes.
- Combine flour, turmeric and rice flour.
- Whisk the egg.
- Tip the dry ingredients into the yeast mixture and beat in the whisked egg or replacer.
- Add the oil and beat the mixture for 1 minute with the electric mixer.

Baking

- Preheat the oven to 180°C (350°F).
- Pour the mixture into the bread pans.
- Leave to stand for 15 minutes.
- Sprinkle with pumpkin seeds.
- Place in the centre of the oven and bake for 15 minutes.
- Remove from the oven and wrap in a clean tea towel to cool.

Sausage-filled Fingers

These buns are filled with gluten-free cocktail sausages. I bake them in éclair trays.

Ingredients

1 cup warm water
1 tsp salt
1 tsp sugar
1 tbsp dried yeast
250g (9oz) Lola's superfine flour
   (page 7)
1 egg white
12 small gluten-free sausages, grilled
sesame seeds for garnish

Preparation

- Grease an éclair tray with margarine and line it with seeds if desired.
- Place the warm water in a bowl and add the salt, sugar and yeast. Let stand for 10 minutes.
- Preheat the oven to 200°C (400°F).

Mixing

- Add the flour, and beat for 1 minute with an electric mixer. Cover and leave to rise until puffy; about 10 minutes. Beat the egg white, add to mixture and beat again for 1 minute.
- Pour a small amount into each prepared tin and top with a sausage.
- Cover with a little more bread batter and let stand to rise for 10 minutes. Sprinkle with seeds.

Baking

- Bake for 10 minutes.

Sultana Snack Bars

Yields four large 80g (2¾in) bars. These great snack bars are ideal for take-out lunches; they will keep at least two weeks in the refrigerator. Rice syrup can be used instead of liquid glucose.

Ingredients

½ cup rolled rice flakes
½ tsp salt
200mL (7fl oz) cold water
½ cup puffed rice
2 tbsp warmed liquid glucose
1 tsp vanilla extract
1 cup sultanas
1 apple, grated
½ cup desiccated coconut
½ cup ground almonds
2 tbsp rice flour
1 tbsp of psyllium

Preparation

- Line a 22 x 8cm (8½ x 3in) bar tin with baking paper.
- Preheat the oven to 150°C (300°F).

Mixing

- Place the rice flakes, salt and cold water into a deep covered casserole dish.
- Microwave on high for 3 minutes.
- Let stand for 3 minutes.
- Add the rice flake mixture to other ingredients.
- Mix well and press into the prepared tin.

Baking

- Bake for 20 minutes.
- Remove from the oven and cut the mixture into four bars.
- Place the cut bars back into the oven on a flat tray and bake for a further 20 minutes, turning once.
- Let cool before wrapping.

Teddy Bear Sandwiches

A school-lunch favourite, these teddy bear-shaped buns are split in two or three pieces to make sandwiches. You will need a set of six teddy tins, so watch out for them in kitchenware shops. One medium-sized potato produces approximately 60g (2oz) mashed potato.

Ingredients

1 tbsp gelatine
200mL (7fl oz) cold water
65g warm mashed potato
65mL (2¼fl oz) olive oil
1 tsp sugar
1 tsp salt
1 tbsp dried yeast
250g (9oz) Lola's superfine flour
    (page 7)
1 egg or equivalent egg replacer
linseeds and a few pieces of walnut
    for garnish.

Preparation

- Place the gelatine in the cold water and let stand to soften.
- Preheat the oven to 200°C (400°F).
- Select a set of six teddy bear tins to cook the buns.
- Grease them heavily with dairy-free margarine.
- Use walnut pieces for a nose and eyes in the bottom of the tin. Linseeds are good for the paws.

Mixing

- When the gelatine has softened heat the mixture until clear.
- Tip the hot gelatine mixture into the mashed potato and mix well.
- Add the olive oil, sugar and salt to this mixture and while it is still warm add the yeast.
- Add the flour, and unbeaten egg or replacer mix.
- Beat the mixture with an electric beater for about 1 minute.
- (The mixture should be a thick batter. Add a little more warm water if too stiff.)
- Pour the batter into the prepared pans and let it stand for 10–15 minutes; it will still continue to rise in the oven.

Baking

- Cook for about 20 minutes or until the buns sound hollow when tapped.

Party Breads

Bruschetta

When we were in Italy I was told this popular treat originated in Tuscany. I find the basic potato bread good for this gluten-free version. It can be made of stale bread and frozen. Finish by grilling before serving. It is best to wrap bruschetta in foil rather than plastic to prevent drying in the freezer.

Ingredients

small amount fresh or dried herbs
finely chopped clove of garlic
salt and pepper to taste
soft butter or margarine
1 gluten-free stock cube
several slices of thick-cut potato
    bread (page 75)

Preparation

- Add the herbs, garlic and seasoning to the butter.
- Crumble the stock cube and work it into the mixture.
- Mix well with a wooden spoon or in a food processor.
- Spread thickly on the bread and toast under a hot griller.

Hint: If you are freezing the bruschetta, join the buttered sides and they will easily separate when defrosted or they can be toasted frozen, in joined pairs, then separated and finished under the griller before serving.

Other toppings

to add to the butter:
sundried tomato, salt and chopped basil
ready-made pesto
bacon, cheese and a little chopped chilli
blue cheese and a drizzle of balsamic vinegar

Traditional Italian bruschetta

- Toast the bread on a griddle pan and brush the top with virgin olive oil, a touch of crushed garlic and coarse salt and finish under a hot grill.

Canapés

These tiny appetisers always attract admiration particularly at a gluten-free function. The bread circles can be cut, buttered and frozen in facing pairs when you have plenty of bread. I make them with my white sandwich loaf, as the fine texture is ideal. Makes 40 canapés.

Preparation

- The sandwich loaf slices are first buttered, and then sandwiched and cut with a small scone cutter, four cuts from a sandwich giving you eight canapés. Five sandwiches giving you 40 canapes.
- If you haven't a small cutter you can cut the sandwiches in tiny squares after removing the crusts.
- Allow at least three per person; they look best on a flat tray arranged in rows of the same type. I have used all types of covers for the tray from paper doilies, crocheted cloths or heavily-greased trays with fronds of maidenhair fern pressed on to it. If you are using doilies it is best to lightly butter the tray to keep the doilies in place.

Assembly

Lay the buttered bread circles in rows on the tray, place a tiny frill of lettuce on one side of the circle on all but one row, use the mint leaves for this row. Pipe or spoon a small dab of cream cheese on the centre to hold the topping steady when they are taken from the tray.

- Row 1 Arrange the prawns /shrimp on cream–cheese–topped lettuce leaves.
- Row 2 Arrange pieces of Camembert cheese on cream–cheese–topped lettuce leaves. Finish with a slice of stuffed olive.
- Row 3 Arrange squares of pâté on cream–cheese–topped lettuce leaves.
- Row 4 Arrange pineapple pieces on cream–cheese–topped mint leaves.
- Row 5 Arrange ham pieces on cream–cheese–topped lettuce leaves.

Top all the canapés with a dab of mayonnaise to hold a tiny piece of parsley, gherkin or olive. Cover the tray with cling wrap or a damp cloth to keep cool until required. Refrigerate if possible. The five rows of eight per row can be complimented with a row of dried apricots filled with sour cream and a piece of crystallised ginger on one side, and a row of prunes filled with a dab of cream cheese to hold a pecan nut on the other side.

Dip-filled Milk Loaf

This dip-filled loaf will astound your coeliac friends. The bread recipe is not important as it is only the crunchy shell of the loaf that you are using, so any recipe could be used as long it was cooked in a tall tin.

Smoked Salmon and Avocado Dip

Ingredients

1 tall milk loaf (page 72)
1 cup sour cream
1 cup cream cheese
2 ripe avocados mashed
juice of half a lime or lemon
½ cup chopped celery
½ cup chopped red capsicum
1 tsp chopped chilli
as much smoked salmon as you wish
note: canned salmon or ham can be
   used if you prefer

Making the dip

- Combine the sour cream and cream cheese and beat until smooth, stir in the mashed avocado and lime juice, add celery, capsicum,chilli and smoked salmon.

Preparation

- Slice off a large lid piece from the patterned loaf bottom to make an attractive top.
- Remove half of the bread from the inside of the loaf.

To serve

- Place the loaf on a large platter and fill with the dip.
- Place the lid on top of the filling.
- Encourage guests to break pieces of the loaf to eat with the dip.
- The loaf can be sliced down a few inches to help.

Croutons and Crumbs

Gluten-free bread is expensive to make so don't waste it.
Make any of these products when you have spare or stale bread.

Fried bread canapes

- Cut slices of gluten-free bread into shapes using heart shaped cutter.
- Lightly fry in olive oil or other light oil and drain on kitchen paper.
- Use as a base for piped cream cheese dip.
- Large circles cut with a scone cutter are used to top french onion soup.

Diced croutons

- Remove crusts from bread slices and cut into cube shapes for use in soups and salads.
- Small croutons are used for soups and larger cubes for salads. Freeze well.

Oven-baked croutons

- Toast slices in toaster until pale golden colour.
- Remove crusts and cut slices into tiny triangles or fingers.
- Preheat oven to 180°C (350°F). Place the toast on a baking tray and bake oven for about 10 minutes.
- Can be kept in a jar or frozen until required. Serve with pâté or dips.

Fresh Crumbs

- Use crusts or bread slices in a food processor or blender to make fresh crumbs for stuffing. Freeze in plastic bags.
- Make sure that they are marked 'gluten-free crumbs'.

Dried Crumbs

- Place bread slices on a tray in a warm oven overnight or after baking to dry out bread for making crumbs.
- Place in food processor to crumb.
- When cool these may be kept in a jar for crumbing cutlets or fish.
- These can be used as a topping instead of cheese add some dairy-free margarine and sprinkle on top of your dish.

Garlic and Herb Breads

Garlic and herb breads freeze well and keep for many months. They are great stand-by for a meal accompaniment or to serve as an appetiser with drinks. Make some whenever you have spare bread, or bake some potato bread in saddle tins and slice down the centre to give you long pieces.

Garlic bread

Ingredients

One loaf of potato bread (see page 75). Cooked in the saddle tin and cut lengthwise it is perfect for this bread.
125g (4½oz) soft margarine or butter
2 cloves of crushed fresh garlic

Preparation

- Blend together the butter and garlic.
- Slice the long pieces of bread in diagonal slices and butter each side with the garlic butter.
- Roll in pieces of aluminium foil and label with date and name.

Herb bread

Preparation

The potato bread can also be used here or you can use one of the easy loaves such as Quick Focaccia in the Flatbread section (see page 116).

- Add fresh chopped herbs to the soft butter if you are going to use the bread immediately or dried mixed herbs if you want to freeze it for many months wrap and label as before.
- The bread can be heated straight from the freezer.
- Tasty or blue cheese can also be used instead of herbs for a different flavour.

Freezing

- Wrap the prepared bread in aluminium foil and label with the date.
- Bread will keep up to 12 weeks in freezer.

Heating

- Preheat oven to 180°C (350°F), heat the frozen bread sticks 20 minutes.
- Thawed or fresh bread sticks require about 10 minutes.

Dip Sticks

These sticks are baked in an éclair or sponge finger tray.
Serve with pâtè or dips.

Ingredients

125ml warm water
1 tsp sugar
1 tsp salt
2 tsp dried yeast
160g (5½oz) Lola's superfine flour
  (page 7)
1 tsp gelatine
2 tbsp olive oil

Preparation

- Place the warm water into a medium-sized mixing bowl.
- Add the sugar, salt and dried yeast, and stir with a fork.
- Leave to stand until the mixture froths, about 5 minutes.
- Grease your sponge finger trays.

Mixing

- Add the remaining dry ingredients to the frothy yeast mixture and whisk well.
- Cover the bowl and set aside to stand for 15 minutes.
- Add the olive oil and whisk again.

Baking

- Preheat the oven to 180°C (350°F).
- Spoon or pipe the mixture into the sponge finger trays.
- Let stand for 10 minutes.
- Cook for 15 minutes.
- Cool and store in an airtight container.

Burger Buns

These buns are cooked in Yorkshire pudding tins to give a real hamburger bun appearance. A flat top is achieved by placing a scone tray on top of the rising loaf 10 minutes into the baking time.

Ingredients

500mL (17½fl oz) warm water
65mL (2¼fl oz) olive oil
1 tbsp glycerine
2 tbsp gelatine
2 tbsp Lola's bread improver
2 tbsp salt
2 tsp sugar
2 tbsp dried yeast
500g (17½oz) Lola's superfine flour (page 7)

Preparation

- Grease the Yorkshire pudding trays with margarine.
- Place all the water, oil and glycerine into large mixing bowl.

Mixing

- Add the dry ingredients to the liquids and mix well for about 1 minute.
- Cover the bowl with a large plastic bag; no need to remove the beater.
- Leave to rise for 10–15 minutes.
- Beat the mixture for 1 minute.
- Preheat the oven to 200°C (400°F).
- Leave the mixture to rise for 20 minutes or less until it is puffy.

Baking

- Bake on the middle shelf for 25 minutes.
- Remove from oven and wrap in a clean tea towel.

Pizza Bases

These bases can be frozen and the topping added as required. Care should be taken to undercook them as they will be cooked again with the topping.

Ingredients

500mL (17½fl oz) warm water
65mL (2¼fl oz) olive oil
2 tbsp gelatine
2 tbsp Lola's bread improver
2 tsp salt
2 tsp sugar
2 tbsp dried yeast
500g (17½oz) Lola's superfine flour
    (page 7)

Preparation

- Cut circles of baking paper to line the bottom of the pizza trays if you are going to
  freeze them or grease the trays for immediate use.

Mixing

- Add the dry ingredients to the liquids and mix well for about 1 minute.
- Cover the bowl with a large plastic bag; no need to remove the beater.
- Leave to rise for 10–15 minutes.
- Beat the mixture again for 1 minute.
- Preheat the oven to 200°C (400°F).
- Spread the mixture thinly on the bases. For a cheese-filled base, spread a layer of batter then a layer of grated cheese then top with more batter.
- Leave to rise for 15 minutes or less until the mixture is puffy.

Baking

- Bake on the middle shelf for 10–15 minutes.
- Remove from oven and wrap in a clean tea towel.

Hors D'oeuvres

Potato bread cooked in a saddle tin will give an attractive oval shape for these delicacies. They can be served for a generous pre-dinner or cocktail party snack or as a first course for a luncheon.

Preparation

- Slice the loaf and spread with a dip or creamed butter to hold the fillings, that should be generously, piled high on the bread.

Suggested toppings

smoked salmon
potato salad
rare roast beef
horseradish and cucumber
smoked chicken
sundried-tomato dip
fresh shelled prawns /shrimp
lettuce with tartare
grilled chicken breast
sliced avocado

Garnishing

The garnish is dependant on the way the hors d'oeuvres are served.
If they are served as finger food, care must be taken to ensure that the garnish does not fall off as the food is lifted from the platter.
A dab of cream cheese will secure parsley or thinly sliced olive or gherkin.
If the breads are served as a first course on a plate at the table, more elaborate garnishes can take the form of salad dressings swirled on the plate with such accompaniments as half strawberries, fresh herbs, watercress or sprouts.
Flowers such as violets or nasturtiums can also be used.

Sandwich Centrepiece

This stunning sandwich centrepiece is particularly appreciated at a coeliac function.

Ingredients

1 gluten-free sandwich loaf (page 73)
soft butter or margarine
1 ripe avocado
100g (4oz) minced or finely chopped
    ham or smoked salmon
3 hard-boiled eggs mashed with
    gluten-free mayonnaise
chopped parsley and cucumber
grated tasty cheese
chicken liver pâté.
smooth low-fat cream (or ricotta)
    cheese
gherkins and stuffed olives for
    garnish

Preparation

I use my sandwich bread recipe for the centrepiece but for a smaller result you can use the small white loaf recipe.

- Place the cooled bread in the freezer for at least an hour before you commence slicing.
- Slice the bread horizontally in about four or five slices; an electric knife is good for this.
- Remove the crusts and butter the slices each side.

Assembly

- Layer the bread slices, fill with different fillings such as avocado mixed with cream cheese; smoked salmon with mayonnaise; mashed egg, grated tasty cheese and chopped parsley or cucumber; and soft chicken liver pâté.
- Finally coat the loaf with the cream cheese and decorate as desired with piped cream rosettes. Garnish with gherkins and stuffed olives.
- Refrigerate for several hours or overnight before cutting in slices to serve.

Machine Breads

A Word From Lola

Dianne Boyle has been researching bread-machine recipes for the Coeliac Society for many years. She has contributed some of her recipes and tips to this chapter.

Hints that may help

COLLAPSED CRUST	This can occur if the loaf is left to rise too long in the final cycle stage.
COURSE TEXTURE	This is due to the dough rising too fast and not being knocked back enough.
DENSE HEAVY LOAF	Insufficient or poor quality yeast or not enough rising time in the last stage. Always use dried instant yeast in bread machines.
INCORRECT MEASUREMENT	This can occur due to cup measurements, as all flour from the same grain does not weigh the same amount. The same cup of flour can vary by up to 30g (1oz) depending on the brand, the texture of the grind and the area it's grown in. This means that your loaf will be too dry to rise properly. For a consistent result weigh your ingredients.
CONSISTENCY	If you are unfamiliar with gluten-free bread cookery you may not realise that gluten-free bread mixture is a batter and not dough like conventional wheaten bread. To obtain a good result your bread mixture should be the consistency of a sponge cake batter or thick custard; a mixture that is too thick cannot allow the yeast to rise.

Improving the result

BREAD IMPROVER	A gluten-free bread improver will help to achieve a finer texture. Beware as many bread improvers contain wheat products.
LESSONS FROM MANUFACTURER	Most manufacturers provide recipe books and some provide lessons in the use of the machine.
GRAIN-LIKE TEXTURE	This can be achieved by the addition of ground sunflower seeds replacing up to 100g (4oz) of the flour. Seeds such as poppy, sesame and linseed can also be used.
FLOUR BLENDS	Different flours blended will give a better flavour than using straight rice flour or tapioca starch. There are many gluten-free products other than those in my recipes that you can try such as buckwheat, amaranth or quinoa.
QUALITY YEAST	Good quality yeast is a most important part of bread-making whether by machine or by conventional mixer methods. I prefer to use instant dried yeast such as Fermipan as commercial bakers have tested it for many years. I find it more tolerant to heat and cold, giving a good result in the tropics or colder climates. During testing of gluten-free cookery I have found it impossible to get a result with some common brands of yeast.

Tips From Dianne Boyle

ASSIST KNEAD

6–8 minutes into the knead cycle, lift lid, do not pause or turn machine off. Using a spatula scrape down sides of tin, mix ingredients until well combined in the same direction as the blade is turning, check corners of tin for dry ingredients. Batter should resemble a medium batter mix or mashed potato. Close lid and allow program to finish.

FLOURS

A blend of flours will give a better result, and a nicer flavour to the bread.

PSYLLIUM

This will give extra elasticity and fibre to the bread—add 2 tablespoons to any of my 1–1.25kg (35¼–44oz) bread recipes, plus an extra 20mL of water.

FRUCTOSE

Add 2 teaspoons of fructose to any of my 1–1.25kg (35¼–44oz) bread recipes; this will improve the rising of the bread.

IMPORTANT

Remove bread from machine within 10 minutes of the completed program.
Make sure that it is cold before slicing.

DI'S BAKING POWDER

This mix will be sufficient for 9–10 loaves.
Weigh into small screw top jar or container:
- 40g (1½oz) white rice flour
- 30g (1oz) cream of tartar
- 50g (2oz) bicarbonate soda
- 30g (1oz) tartaric acid

Place lid on container and shake well.

Lola's Brown Fruit Loaf

Ingredients

500mL (17½fl oz) warm water
1 tbsp warm treacle
3 tbsp dried yeast
2 tsp salt
2 tbsp sugar
4 egg beaten egg whites
65mL (2¼fl oz) olive oil
500g (17½oz) Lola's superfine flour
  (page 7)
1 tbsp glycerine
100g (4oz) mixed dried fruits
1 tbsp gelatine
100g (4oz) tapioca starch
1 tbsp carob
1 tsp citric acid
2 tbsp psyllium
1 tbsp parisian essence

Settings

Large loaf/dark crust.
Knead 10 minutes slow + 30 minutes fast.
Rise 15 minutes.
Knock back 30 seconds.
Rise 25 minutes.
Bake 98 minutes.

Method

- Set cycle according to detail above.
- Place the warm water and treacle in the pan; add yeast, salt and sugar and let stand while you weigh other ingredients and beat the egg whites.
- Add beaten egg whites and oil to the ingredients in the pan.
- Tip in flour and remainder of ingredients.
- Start cycle.
- Scrape down after 5 minutes then leave to complete cycle.
- When cold, slice and pack in plastic bag to retain moisture.

Lola's Seeded White Loaf

There is more yeast used in gluten-free loaves that do not contain xanthan gum, but yeast is much cheaper than gum. This is a large delicious loaf.

Ingredients

600mL (21fl oz) warm water
3 tbsp dried yeast
2 tsp salt
1 tbsp sugar
4 beaten egg whites
¼ cup olive oil
500g (17½oz) Lola's superfine flour
   (page 7)
100g (4oz) arrowroot
1 tbsp gelatine
½ tsp citric acid
2 tbsp psyllium
3 tbsp mixed seeds; poppy, sesame
   & linseed
1 tbsp amaranth cereal

Settings

Large loaf/dark crust.
Knead 10 minutes slow + 30 minutes fast.
Rise 15 minutes.
Knock back 30 seconds + 30 seconds.
Rise 25 minutes. Bake 98 minutes.

Method

- Set cycle according to detail above.
- Place the warm water in the pan; add yeast, salt and sugar and let stand while you weigh other ingredients and beat the egg whites.
- Add beaten egg whites and oil to the ingredients.
- Tip in flour and remainder of ingredients.
- Start cycle.
- Scrape down after 5 minutes then leave to complete cycle.
- When cold, slice and pack in plastic bag to retain moisture.

Dianne Bakes Yeast-free

Wet ingredients

Place these ingredients straight into
    baking pan
1/3 cup light olive oil
3 medium eggs, approximately 60g
    (2oz) each
480–500mL (17–17½fl oz) tepid
    water

Dry ingredients

Weigh into flexible plastic container
    (ice cream container)
375g (13oz) white rice flour
125g (4½oz) arrowroot or tapioca
    flour
110g brown rice flour
60g (2oz) besan flour
3 tsp Di's baking powder (page 157)
1½ tsp bicarbonate of soda
3 tsp cream of tartar
1 tbsp sugar
1 tbsp xanthan gum
1 tsp salt

Settings

Dark crust.
This loaf needs a long bake.
Use Yeast-free setting if available or Wholewheat Rapid.
Loaf size: 1–1.25kg (35¼–44oz).

Method

- Roughly mix all dry ingredients with a hand whisk.
- Pull container corner to corner to form spout—it makes tipping
    into bread pan easier
- Tip dry ingredients into bread pan on top of wet ingredients.
- Assist knead 5–7 minutes into knead cycle (see page 157).
- Place the pan in the machine and commence cycle.
- Leave bread in machine for 10 minutes when baking cycle has
    finished—no longer.
- Remove bread from machine. Cool in tin for 5 minutes before
    turning out onto rack.
- Slice when cool.
- Freezes well.

Dianne's Light White Loaf

Wet ingredients

¹/₃ cup light olive oil
3 medium-sized eggs
450–470ml (15¾–16½fl oz) tepid
  water
1 tsp white wine vinegar

Dry ingredients

430g (15oz) white rice flour
110g (3¾oz) arrowroot
130g (3½oz) potato flour
½ tbsp white sugar
1 tbsp xanthan gum
1½ tsp salt
3 tsp dried yeast
2 tsp fructose

Settings

Dark crust.
Use Turbo or Basic.
Use loaf size: 1–1.25kg (35¼–44oz).

Method

- Place all ingredients into bread pan in order given, starting with wet ingredients.
- Set program, place bread in machine, close lid, push start.
- Assist knead 5–7 minutes into knead cycle.
- When baking is complete remove bread pan from machine within 10 minutes.
- Leave to cool in tin for 5–10 minutes before turning out.
- Slice when cool.
- Freezes well.

Dianne's Rice and Besan Bread

Variation: ½ cup of grated cheese can be added after the arrowroot.

Wet ingredients

480–500mL (17–17½fl oz) warm
    water
480–500mL (17–17½fl oz) warm
    water
3 x 60g (2oz) eggs
80ml olive oil
1 tsp white vinegar

Dry ingredients

180g brown rice flour
270g white rice flour
140g (5oz) arrowroot
80g besan flour
2 tbsp psyllium
2 tsp fructose
1 tbsp sugar
1 tbsp xanthan gum
1½ tsp salt
2 tsp dried yeast
3 tbsp milk powder (optional: plus
    extra 15ml water)

Settings

Use Basic Rapid or Turbo–select dark crust or Wholewheat-Rapid–
select medium crust.
Use loaf size: 1–1.25kg.

Method

- Place all ingredients in bread pan in listed order starting with
  wet ingredients.
- Set program, place pan in machine, close lid, press start 6-8
  minutes into cycle – assist knead (page 154).
- Close lid and complete the cycle.
- Remove bread from machine within 10 minutes of the
  completed program.
- Stand for 5 minutes in pan before turning out to cool.
- Cool before slicing.

Freezing

This loaf can be frozen and thawed in the microwave before use.
1 minute on high heat for a frozen slice. It is better to slightly
overheat it to give a softer texture.

Conversion Table

All spoon measurements are level.

Approximate quantities rounded to usable units

Metric cup measures are available in most countries; it is advisable to use them instead of guessing or using a kitchen cup. The conversion quantities given are approximate, rounded to the most practical unit; they are not as accurate as the metric measurements. My recipes use the tablespoon that is 20g (^{2}/$_3$oz) . Beware that American tablespoons measure 15g, so an additional level teaspoon of the ingredient must be used to achieve the same result.

LIQUIDS
1 metric cup = 250mL (9fl oz)
½ metric cup = 125mL (4fl oz)
⅓ metric cup =   80mL (2½fl oz)
¼ metric cup =   65mL (2¼fl oz)

SPOONS
1 teaspoon = 5g
1 tablespoon = 20g (^{2}/$_3$oz)

DRY INGREDIENTS
50g = approximately 2 oz
100g = approximately 4 oz
250g = approximately 8½ oz
450g = approximately 16 oz

OVEN TEMPERATURE
140°C / 275°F / gas mark 1
160°C / 325°F / gas mark 3
180°C / 350°F / gas mark 4
200°C / 400°F / gas mark 6
240°C / 475°F / gas mark 9

Index